A Pair of Cranks

A Pair of Cranks

A compendium of essays by two of the most influential and challenging authors of the 20th century.

Leopold Kohr
E.F. Schumacher

Edited with an Introduction by **John Papworth**

Published in the United Kingdom in 2003 by

New European Publications Limited
14-16 Carroun Road
London SW8 1JT, England

British Library Cataloguing in Publication Data

ISBN 1-872410-18-9

Cover and page design   info@orbitgraphic.co.uk

Printed and bound in Great Britain by Antony Rowe, Chippenham, Wiltshire.

Contents

Introduction

John Papworth

The authors whose work fills this volume were fully aware of the imposing economic and political realities which dominate our lives and which increasingly threaten us with nemesis, and in this they could claim some degree of uniqueness; for years they were lone voices promoting a radically new perspective in seeking to grapple with them. They did not join any political party, they did not campaign for 'peace', or to 'ban the bomb', or for lower taxes or for higher welfare handouts; however desirable or necessary in themselves such things might be; instead they focussed their energies on what they regarded as the supremely important issue of the contemporary scene, and on a factor nearly all other politically engaged persons chose to disregard, or of which they might have had no awareness.

Their concern was focussed on the factor of size, and given the extent to which measurement dominates so many aspects of life, the prevailing disregard of it in relation to political and economic institutions was and is surely remarkable. After all, a fraction of an inch either way in the size of a shoe means it either pinches or tends to slip off; the size of a garden spade must be appropriate to the size of the person using it; the size of a toothbrush needs to be related to the size of human dental arrangements and so on. But in politics and economics this factor is either not considered or pushed into the background of other considerations regardless of the consequences – which are often disastrous. This perspective of the singular importance of size and scale is at last beginning to find wider acceptance, and this major shift of consciousness is one of the most hopeful auguries of contemporary developments.

The first on the scene of the new radical thinking was Leopold Kohr. An Austrian by birth, after studying at the universities of Innsbruck, Paris and Vienna he escaped the probable destiny of one of Hitler's death camps and during the war was in charge of a Customs Union research project in Washington. His book, *The Breakdown of Nations*, after being hawked around the publishing world repeatedly, was finally published by Faber and Faber in 1957, largely owing to the intervention of one of its directors, the well-known poet Sir Herbert Read.

The publication date is worth some attention: nearly half a century ago perhaps one of the most important political treatises of the 20th century first saw daylight. It was only sketchily reviewed and even then in largely dismissive or patronising terms, and but for the efforts of some perceptive supporters, might well have sunk without trace. Its thesis found no acceptance in any party political programme, nor did it appear to merit any attention in any university teaching programme, a situation which, despite the formidable changes of recent decades and the spur to new thinking they have given, still appears to hold.

This is not the place for a detailed analysis of its theme but we may care to note that it begins with an examination of many of the contemporary explanations for the major troubles of the time, that they are due to war, economic upheavals and collapse, unemployment and other aspects of social misery, and each explanation in turn is dismissed as a prelude to introducing his own explanation in terms of size. He does this by referring back to Aristotle:

To the size of a state there is a limit, as there is to plants, animals and implements, for none of these retain their natural facility when they are too large.

From there he goes on to explain how none of the problems confronting the modern world can be successfully tackled if the signpost of its concluding phrase and Aristotle's overall message are ignored. It is a message Kohr proceeded to apply with a wit and profundity all too rare in modern political literature but, as already indicated, at the time it found few takers.

Fritz Schumacher was almost an exact contemporary of Kohr; both were of German speaking origins, both were economists and both were primarily concerned with the factor of size as being the key to grasping the real nature of, as well as the real solution to, the problems of contemporary life.

Schumacher's book, *Small is Beautiful*, by contrast with Kohr's *Breakdown of Nations*, was an instant success. It first appeared nearly twenty years later and sold by the million, as well as giving its author an international reputation. It might be thought that a major publishing event of this order would have had a considerable influence on party political programmes, on government policies and not least on university teaching, but the evidence that it did so is hard to find. Its theme was of course, despite its absurd title, similar to Kohr's, but whereas the latter had expounded a systematic thesis, Schumacher's book was largely a collation of articles written at different times for different purposes. Their main burden was indeed that of questioning the prevailing acceptance of the ideas of size and more significantly, the acceptance of growth as being both a feasible and worthy objective, and the promotion of practical alternatives.

Kohr appears to have had no orthodox religious views, whereas Schumacher eventually embraced Catholicism and this is reflected in much of his writings, not least in *Small is Beautiful*. What follows in these pages from the pens of both is a roving camera of comment on different aspects of the global crisis but always from the perspective of the factor of scale and, in this case, the human scale, from two quite different temperaments.

They consist of articles contributed to two journals the present author founded and edited, the first of which, *Resurgence*, originally subtitled *The Journal of The Fourth World*, both writers helped me to establish, and the second, *Fourth World Review*, established after Schumacher's untimely demise in 1977, to which Kohr was a regular contributor until his death in 1994. The question may well be asked, "Why republish them now?" and to this there are several answers. One is that their intrinsic merit is its own recommendation for wider reader attention; another is that the problems both authors seek to grapple with are now of even graver import than when they wrote, if only because the basic structural causes continue to be ignored.

But a third answer is probably more compelling: the failure of orthodox remedies to resolve the elements of the global crisis has had its own significant impact on public consciousness. We are today at the beginning of the 21st Century in a quite different world from that which prevailed around the middle of the 20th.

At that time to question the structure of political and economic reasoning was to invite ridicule, abuse or indifference; people who did so were so obviously cranks and in no way merited serious attention. Today such attitudes are significantly less strident, the gathering clouds of global prospects are conveying their own message. (Does the reader need to be reminded of the new world war waiting to happen as a result of the accelerating armaments programmes around the world? Or of the inevitable global economic collapse that will ensue from the current mindless pursuit of 'growth' in a world of finite resources? Of the monstrous depravity of our assaults on the life-support systems of the planet? Or of the multiplying evidence of individual stress and of family and social breakdown now proliferating in all 'developed' countries?). At last people are being impelled to question assumptions which formerly held unquestioned sway.

Not least we need to note the upsurge of ethnic and regional nationalism which today has become one of the most dynamic features of the political scene. The pressure for Scottish and Welsh self-government is mirrored by similar moves for localised independence everywhere, constituting a ferment now global in its scope and which is going to compel continuous map redrawing for generations to come.

And of course this ferment is in full accord with what both Kohr and Schumacher spent much of their adult lives seeking to promote. Yet if it is one thing to propose change, especially in some fundamental matters, it is another to be involved in it when one may lack a clear grasp of the deeper reasons why a change of course is needed at all.

A journey without clear signposts can be a hazardous business and likely to result in much confusion and a multiplicity of cross purposes which may lead nowhere. What follows here is precisely the kind of material the modern radical so often needs in order to get his bearings in seeking worthwhile results. Amid a plethora of political literature this volume can claim its own priority for attention, not least from the extent to which time has amply confirmed the validity of the principles to which it relates and which both authors did so much to expound.

The catchphrase 'Small is Beautiful' had the merit of striking a responsive chord in the general consciousness enough to make Schumacher's book, of which it was the title, one of global appeal. But for many thinking people there was a downside in that it smacked of sentiment rather than reality, of a yearning for an unreal and unrealisable world rather than addressing the imposing problems of here and now. Besides it embodied a patent untruth, small can also, like a nail in ones shoe, a torture chamber, a cesspit or a bee sting be painful, abhorrent or ugly. It is a consideration which may help to explain why the concept has found so little expression in the formulation of official policies.

Such influence as it may have had in 'radical', 'green' or 'alternative' thinking also seems to have declined markedly from its initial impetus. A document issued by 'Positive News' and the Schumacher Society in August 2002 projects a nine point programme which makes no direct reference to the basic tenets of the Kohr/Schumacher theoretical concerns at all.

One purpose in publishing these essays is to convey just how solid, authoritative and far reaching is the reasoning that buttresses the whole concept, and its starkly practical relevance to the problems of social organisation that beset us today. The reader will find here a vigorous analytical approach to such matters as land, money, labour, farming, urban slums, war, economic malaise and Third World poverty. In each case he will find a fresh perspective being applied to old problems, a perspective which is scholarly and clear-sighted, as well as challenging to established assumptions over a wide field.

Hence the purpose of this important volume is not simply to produce a recycling of former contributions to two journals in which they first appeared, but to furnish the radical movement with a reminder of some vitally important theoretical equipment it currently conspicuously lacks, written by two of the most important political writers of the 20th Century.

Both had a common theme, but as we have noted, they approached their work from widely differing perspectives. Leopold Kohr was a polymath whose writings express a familiarity not only with the abstruse reaches of economics, a subject in which he held a professorship in the University of Puerto Rico, but in political theory reaching back to classical authors of ancient Greece, and also in the world of modern physics, mathematics, art and literature. The sheer breadth and depth of his learning found ready expression in the fund of examples and allusions on which he was able to draw to give, repeatedly, illumination and arresting insights to the theories he was propounding.

His major work was indubitably *The Breakdown of Nations*, which must have been in gestatation in the late thirties and early forties of the last century. Despite the awe-inspiring tragedies of

two world wars, economic upheavals and the malignant dicta-
torships of Hitler and Stalin, the radical world still lacked any
awareness of the true nature of its problems. In Britain and
elsewhere, the easy assumption still dominated left-wing
thinking that all that was needed to solve the problems of war
and economic malaise was a change of centralised government.
There was no hint in any of its publications, especially in *The
New Statesman*, and in the stream of pamphlets put out by the
Fabian Society, in the hey-day of both (and both were leading, if
not indeed, dominant, voices of the period), that what was
required was not so much a change of government as a change
in the *scale* of government.

So the solutions advanced by socialist thinkers generally did
not reach beyond a belief that schemes for the nationalisation of
industry, of health care, transport, education, social services,
marketing and so on, if adopted, would pave the way to a brave
new world. It was overlooked that a change of government of
this order was simply institutionalising and enlarging the very
scale which was such a major feature of the capitalist world, and
that since the problem lay not so much with capitalism, or
indeed with communism or socialism *per se*, as the scale on
which they operated, that any change which ignored the factor
of scale would run into precisely the same problems.

And so it has proved and today, over sixty years later, the
same problems beset whatever government is in power, in
whatever country, as though neither of the authors with which
here we are concerned had written a word.

It is difficult to recapture the animated spirit for progress
and peace which suffused the 1945 election in which for the first
time a majority UK Labour government with an enormous
majority swept into power. Bliss was it that dawn to be alive! A
socialist commonwealth was going to be created in which all the
old problems, unemployment, inadequate education, poor
health standards, meagre social and welfare provision, would be
swept away and if the reader seeks answers to the problem of

why these phenomena are still with us he may be assured he will find at least some of them in these pages.

If the claim may appear excessive let the reader reflect on the multiple tragedy which was created by the same inflated misconceptions that the Labour government of 1945 inflicted on the then British colonial world. If centralised administration, and much more of it, was good enough for the British people, so official thinking went, it would certainly solve the problems of the colonial world.

But there was a difference, and it was one ignored with wanton official obtuseness, for whereas the varying regions of Britain had been compressed into rule under a single governing body for centuries, the different tribes and small nations of the colonial world had been robbed of their independence and power of self-rule by the much more recent advent of colonial overlordship. Their spirit of independent identity was still very much alive and was generally the motivating force working for freedom from colonial rule.

Not unnaturally they anticipated that with the departure of the colonialists, their dreams of a restoration of free, independent self-government would be realised. Instead they found they had been cruelly betrayed; instead of freedom they found they had merely changed one set of overlords for another.[1]

The colonialists took care to hand over power based on their own presuppositions of centralised administration and control, and a book describing how this was done in the teeth of the bitter opposition of the local tribal and hereditary royal leaders and the consequences which ensued, has yet to be written. Their struggle was little reported in the press, the organs of which were far more concerned to report the emergence of the new forms of colonial rule now in the hands of indigenous leaders elected in accordance with the bogus democratic procedures that were current in the homelands of the departing colonial powers.[2]

What was fully reported subsequently was the inevitable orgy of violent fratricidal conflict which erupted in many parts in the wake of the demise of the former colonial rulers. In Africa the toll of human life now runs into millions. Scarcely any part of the continent has escaped the inevitable strife that the neglect of the centuries-old tribal institutions has provoked and today, for the most part, it has become a huge arena of endemic misrule, corruption and oppression as it sinks to ever lower levels of poverty and social disintegration. It is a tragedy as vast as it is needless and if the principles enunciated in many of the following essays had been heeded there is little doubt it could largely have been avoided.

If the burden of this volume is concerned with the more immediate and imposing problems confronting the survival prospects of civilisation generally, and more especially in the more advanced mis-developed countries, it is because those problems are here more pronounced. And the overall problem abides, what is the direction our affairs need to take and how do we go about taking it? Of one thing we may be sure, and it is an unspoken affirmation that runs throughout these pages, that attempts to grapple with the problems of the modern world which ignore the factor of scale are predestined to fail because it is precisely such ignoring which has done so much to create the problems in the first place.

It does not follow that if this factor is taken fully into account all our problems will just disappear. We are not perfect beings and there are no perfect solutions to the problems of seeking an harmonious, equitable, peaceful and free society, especially in a context where some forms of global association are already operating; all that can be affirmed is that if it is adopted we will cease to be helpless in seeking to grapple with them; that they will, in many important respects, become manageable and containable, whereas the forces promoting them are now running amok, out of control and defying any attempts to restrain them.

The references of many of these essays relate for the most part to the period in which they were written – the third quarter of the 20th century, but however dated, the principles they are used to expound represent significant advances in the field of human understanding and development. As such they are part of the heritage of human wisdom which no one concerned with the matters of under discussion can afford to neglect.

They are of singular importance for the way they help to provide a significant part of the theoretical basis of the world revolution now happening under our noses. They are pointing to the world of tomorrow, a world which will not be in pawn to a few megalomaniac 'great' powers, but in the free hands of a rapidly growing number of small, often minuscule, independent nations. These nations will cooperate in a variety of ways that serve their common interests as common sense suggests they should, but it will not be a world dominated by EUrope, China, America or any other super-power-entity, and if it survives on a human scale basis, survives too the current US propensity for war, and the other threats of power-out-of-control such as nuclear power, GM crops, economic collapse, sheer excess of human numbers, environmental degradation or social disintegration, we may yet make some advances in realising the age-old human dream of freedom, justice and sanity.

JOHN PAPWORTH
August 2002

1 A Fabian pamphlet written by Marjorie Nicholson and published in 1948 presents perhaps the general core of Fabian thinking then and as it prevails to this day. Entitled *Self-Government and the Communal Problem* it was subtitled *A Study of Colonial Constitutional Problems Arising in Plural Societies.* By 'plural' she is referring to the composition of different territories then part of the British Empire and "how self-government is to be achieved in a colony where the population is divided within itself, whether by race, or nationality or religion". In 45 pages she finds no room to mention the name of a single tribe of any indigenous nation in any territory she discusses.

2 Those who are still persuaded that these procedures based on mass balloting express a genuinely democratic process may like to consult the present writer's *Small is Powerful* (London: New European Publications, 1995), especially chapter 9, where the reality of the democratic content of a process dominated by centrally controlled mass membership parties is analysed in some detail.

Chapter One

A Pair of Cranks!

Leopold Kohr

Ever since E.F. (Fritz) Schumacher's 'Small is Beautiful' was published in Fall 1973, a few months after the delivery of his lecture at the University of Puerto Rico, I have been told that my own ideas sounded very much like his. Of course, because my dear late friend Fritz's ideas sounded very much like mine. The fact is that I was already propagating my theory of size (of small size that is) in the early Forties when Schumacher was still steeped deep in Keynsianism! My first piece on the virtue of smallness appeared in the New York Catholic weekly *The Commonweal* on September 26, 1941 under the title *Disunion Now*, its two subheadings reading: *Cantonal Sovereignty* and *Glorifying the Small.*

At the Boston Convention of the American Economics Association in 1951, when growthmanship had reached the apogee of its career, I gave an unscheduled talk on the invitation of its President-Elect Harold Innes of Toronto (subsequently published in the summer-1956 issue of Canada's *Business Quarterly*) to a sceptical audience of fellow academics on the Limits to Growth – 21 years before the appearance of Professor D.L. Meadows prestigious M.I.T. team-report of 1972 which he had prepared under the same (since then famous) title for the Club of Rome's *Project on the Predicament of Mankind.*

I followed this up with the books *The Breakdown of Nations,* first published in 1957 but written in 1949, *The Overdeveloped Nations* (1962) and *Development Without Aid* (1973), besides a great many articles in English, Italian, Spanish, German, Welsh, Japanese, all dealing with the (until then) totally neglected problems of excessive size. Even Austin Robinson's *The Economic Consequences of the Size of Nations* (1960) barely touched on the subject beyond noting the distinguished Cambridge Professor's "feeling of incredulity" that nearly 200 years after Adam Smith's *The Wealth of Nations,* he was unable "to discover a volume of antecedent literature such as the subject seemed to have deserved" (though *The Breakdown of Nations* had by then already been on the shelves of Cambridge University Library for a full three years).

By this I do not mean to suggest that either Schumacher or myself copied from each other any more than Wallace copied from Darwin.

My system was already complete when Schumacher's began. But coming from different realms of thought and experience, we both developed it independently before we met in John Papworth's similarly inspired newly founded magazine *Resurgence,* which offered us such generous space that readers referred to it as the *Kohr-Schumacher Axis.* Actually, it was also very much John's.

I often compared Fritz and myself to the pair of Siamese twins who, during my Innsbruck student days, were discovered by a Bavarian photographer for the benefit of an April 1 issue of the pre-Hitler Munich satirical weekly *Simplicissimus.* The remarkable singularity about these twins was that they were joined not by their shoulders or hips but had grown together by their beards. The Siamesian phenomenon could therefore develop only in later years, after the twins had reached the appropriate age. If my beard started growing a little earlier, it simply was that I was a little older, and, as I said, if afterwards I sounded like Schumacher, it was because Schumacher sounded like me.

The difference between us was one of emphasis. Schumacher's was on *Intermediate Technology* – small tools, mine on *Appropriate Size* – small nations. In addition he had at his disposal an overwhelming store of statistical material and practical know-how which not only enabled him to predict in the early Sixties the almost terminal fuel crisis of the Seventies but also made him into a top-rate economic adviser. He not only preached but also acted. He founded the London-based *Institute of Intermediate Technology* and then put his own teachings to the test as when he baked in three hours every Sunday a week's supply of bread for his biblically large family. When asked by a lady during his Puerto Rican lecture: "OK, but what does your wife say after your messing-up the kitchen?" he answered: "Lady, when I leave the kitchen, no one knows that anyone has been there." All *I* could ever do was broil steaks which, in the end, gave me gout.

And finally: Fritz had faith. He thought it took three generations for an idea to take roots. I am more inclined to think as Keynes did when he said in the Thirties that in 25 years time his ideas would be accepted by every Treasury in the world. (They were). But by then, he added, "they will not only be obsolete but dangerous" (They are). So, while Schumacher had faith, I have my greatest doubts that any politician (or ordinary citizen for that matter) will ever accept an idea merely because it makes sense – at least to a horse.

Lastly: One might also have compared the twinship of our philosophies with "a double cherry, seeming parted but yet an union in partition." But though the image is Shakespeare's, it is too lyrical to fit two economists thought for the major part of their lives to be cranks, which neither of us ever resented. For as Schumacher put it in answer to a suspicious heckler's question: "What is a crank? A tool that is simple, small, cheap, economical, efficient, easy to handle, and", as he added with emphasis, "it makes revolutions". And this is what few are as yet able to grasp: that the revolution in store for our age will not be by the left against the right, young against old, black against white, but of small against big. As Hamlet might put it were he to monologuise today: "To be small or not to be at all, *that* is the question."

Chapter Two

Man Need Not Starve

E. F. Schumacher

This important article was written in 1966 some of its references date, but the underlying principles need to be seen in the context of events now happening nearly forty years later. In Africa alone the fate of starvation is an imminent reality for millions and two relatively new factors are affecting the peril which the author does not mention. One is climatic vagaries arising from the phenomenon of global warming, which is related to the current crop failure throughout large areas of Eastern Africa, and the other is the appalling devastation of AIDS now affecting a third or more of the people of several African countries.

The World Food Problem has hit the headlines again, and rightly so. World population in 1965 rose by another seventy million, while world food production has remained stationary. The headlines talk about "The World Hunger Gap – Shock Report", and the report in question, entitled 'The State of Food and Agriculture, 1966', comes from the Food and Agriculture Organisation of the United Nations. Its central message is that food availability per head of the world's population has fallen by two percent during last year. But this is not the crux of the story. Food production in the developing countries has dropped by four to five percent per head, and it is they who are really short. The fact that North American production has risen by about four percent and Western European production by one percent does little to improve the situation, except statistically.

Looking behind the surface of things, we find a dramatic change in the world food situation: the North American grain surpluses are running out. The large shipments of American grain to the developing countries did not come out of current production but out of stocks accumulated since the 1950's. These stocks have now fallen to their lowest level in fourteen years; at fifteen million tons, they are said to be not enough for adequate protection against a domestic crop failure. *Time* reports in its issue of 12th August, 1966, that "the supply of soybeans, the dull yellow seed that goes into everything from vegetable oil to paint and constitutes the world's cheapest source of protein, equals just four months' consumption. Five years ago, Government warehouses were jammed with butter and cheese; now they have none. Washington has had to go into the market to buy dried milk for its program of free school lunches for 50 million children in 52 foreign countries."

In August, 1966, the US State Department told American embassies that aid shipments of wheat would have to be cut by 25 percent, and Mr. Orville Freeman, the US Secretary for Agriculture, declared that "unless the hungry nations learn to feed themselves, there will be world famine in less than twenty years". He also said that "more human lives hang in the balance than have been lost in all the wars of history". If anything, he may have understated the seriousness of the situation by talking about the world as a whole. Food supplies do not and cannot 'average out'. The danger of famine in the developing countries is much nearer than "less than twenty years": it is here already. It is unlikely that there will be famine in North America, the Argentine, Australia or the Soviet Union, or indeed in many smaller countries like Rumania or Burma. No, the problem is much more concentrated than that and therefore much more urgent than world averages suggest.

The world food problem, of course, is closely allied to the world population problem; but here again it is not the rise in the total that is really significant. There are many countries, large and small, where further large increases in population will do no harm at all and may even be beneficial. What is really significant is that of the seventy million increase last year some fifty million accrued to the population of particular developing countries which are unable to cope. Neither people nor food will 'average out'.

Let us look at the proposition that 'food does not average out'. People say that it does not make sense to have restrictions on food production in America or Europe when there are starving millions in India. All right, if it does not make sense, can we get a more sensible world? By letting the North American plains produce food for India? This sounds simple enough, but how is India going to pay for it? If she cannot pay, the food has to go as aid. How, then, is the North American farmer to make a living? He would have to be paid by the American taxpayer through the American Government. Is this a feasible long-term proposition? I think not. In a short-term emergency, anything is possible and anything will do. But as a permanent way of life it seems to me to go against the most basic laws of human nature that the population in one part of the world should be maintained free of charge by the population in another part of the world. It is man's first task and duty to feed himself, either directly from his own soil or indirectly by way of trade.

Aid makes sense only if it is conducive to development, not if it merely supports a basically unsupportable situation. What should ever come of such an arrangement? Do you think that permanently, as a matter of world planning, the Indians or the Egyptians or whoever it might be could be pensioned off, as it were, to live on the work and effort of the people of another nation? No man can be free and maintain any kind of self-respect if he cannot even feed himself, directly or indirectly. This, I think, is an unalterable law of human nature, and we must dismiss from our minds any notion of a world with food aid as a permanent feature.

It is interesting to look at the statistics on world food movements with these thoughts in mind. The most relevant food items are grains because they are easily transportable in bulk. Before the war, intercontinental grain shipments amounted to about twenty-four million tons a year, and all of this went to Western Europe which had the means to pay for it. In 1964/65, intercontinental grain shipments amounted to sixty million tons, a tremendous increase. Europe took much the same as before, some twenty-four million tons. New purchasers were the Soviet Union and China, taking a similar amount and being able to pay for it. But a further amount of over twenty million tons went to Asia and Africa as aid. Now this aid food will progressively diminish and probably fadeout altogether. It had come out of stocks, and it seemed good business to turn these stocks, if not into cash, at least into aid. As the stocks disappear, so food aid will disappear and only trade will survive. This is the new situation which the developing world will have to face.

A certain intercontinental division of labour as between agriculture and industry will no doubt continue, and the rich countries which cannot feed themselves from their own soil will continue to be able to send industrial goods overseas so that overseas farmers will produce for them. But will the poor countries, the so-called developing countries, be able to obtain significant amounts of food in exchange for industrial exports? I should think that to produce food for internal consumption will almost invariably be easier for a developing country than to produce industrial products competitively for export, to pay for food imports. There may be exceptions – there always are – but as a general proposition this is an obvious truth. For many years to come, it will be utopian to think that arrangements could be made so that developing countries could become large exporters of industrial goods to, say, the United States, so as to be able to pay for large food imports from North America, or that they would make such exports to Europe, while Europe exported to America, so that American food could flow to the developing world. In short, Mr. Orville Freeman is undoubtedly right when he says that the hungry nations must learn to feed themselves. If they do not do so there may not be *world* hunger but *they* will starve, and this will not come to pass in twenty years but almost right away. Of course, this could have unpleasant effects on the countries – mainly Western Europe and Japan – which have for long been feeding themselves by trade. The 'terms of trade' might change against them, so that they have to give more man-ufactured goods for their food imports: but there is no reason to fear that these countries will starve, because they are rich enough to pay. They have, moreover, the possibility to improve further upon their own agricultural performance, possibly to the point of self-sufficiency in food.

If this general line of argument is accepted, we can move on to the crucial question: *can* the hungry nations feed themselves? Is it possible? Have they got enough land? Can they develop enough productivity? And here we come to a vital question: what do we mean when we say 'productivity'? I apologise if the points I am going to make may seem too simple, but it is often the most simple things that are most confused. When we talk of productivity in connection with the world food problem, the problem of hunger in developing countries, we are primarily talking about *productivity per acre* and not about *productivity per man*. Unless we keep this distinction constantly in mind, we shall get everything mixed up. A given population with a given amount of land will have enough to eat if the output per acre is sufficient to feed them, irrespective of whether a quarter, or half, or 90 percent of the population are actually working on the land. If the output per acre is insufficient they will starve, even if the *productivity per man* is so high that only ten percent of the population are needed for work on the land.

Let us see, therefore, which countries have the highest agricultural productivity in terms of output per acre. To measure the overall productivity of land is a difficult business, and the best statistics available are probably those produced by the Food and Agriculture Organisation of the United Nations. Of the twelve countries shown with the highest productivity per acre classified as agricultural land, in 1956-60, six were in Europe – the Netherlands, Belgium, Denmark, Federal Republic of Germany, Norway and Italy; three were in the Far East – Nationalist China (Taiwan), Japan, and Republic of Korea; two were in South East Asia – Malaya and Ceylon; and one in the near East – the United Arab Republic. While statistics of this kind must not be taken too literally, they give valuable indications. It is interesting to note that the productivity per acre in the United Kingdom is shown as only one-half that of Germany, a third that of Belgium, and a quarter that of the United Arab Republic, and that that of the United States is shown as only about one-half that of the United Kingdom.

Now let us look at the other end of the scale, the dozen countries with the lowest overall productivity per acre. There are two of what used to be called the White dominions – Australia and South Africa; six countries in Latin America – Venezuela, Mexico, Argentine, Uruguay, Brazil, and Honduras; and four countries in Africa – Tunisia, Algeria, Morocco, and Ethiopia. The productivity gap between the 'highest' and the 'lowest' is as much as one to forty.

The ranking order of countries when it comes to productivity *per man*, i.e., per man engaged in agriculture, is of course entirely different. Whilst Australia has the lowest productivity per acre, its productivity per man is among the highest, and Korea, with its very high productivity per acre, is among the countries with the lowest productivity per man. There is no correlation between these two ranking orders, neither positive nor negative;

for productivity per man correlates with the general wealth of the country, whereas productivity per acre correlates (if only to some extent) with the country's density of population.

All this goes to emphasise the importance of distinguishing these two measures of productivity – per acre and per man. As there is absolutely no positive correlation between them, you can imagine what confusion results when people fail to keep them apart.

One fact, at least, stands out: in a poor country a high output per acre is obtainable only through high labour intensity, as in Korea, or Taiwan. This is hardly surprising, because *something* has to be applied to the land to make things grow, and if the country is poor it has little capital to apply to the land; it has only labour power. If it does not go in for labour intensive cultivation, it will certainly not obtain high outputs per acre.

If we talk about the problem of hunger, we must talk primarily about productivity, or output, *per acre*. If we wished to discuss rural poverty, we would have to talk about productivity, or output, *per man*. Hunger and poverty, although they often go together in towns, are easily distinguishable as regards the rural population. A lot of farmers and small cultivators in developing countries are desperately poor, but not necessarily hungry. It is often quite easy to increase the productivity *per man* at the expense of the productivity *per acre*. This may alleviate poverty but does nothing to solve the problem of hunger. It is often also quite easy to increase the output per acre at the expense of labour productivity. This helps to feed the hungry but does nothing to alleviate the poverty of the cultivators. The best, of course, is to raise both productivities, – but where it is a matter of choice it must never be forgotten that the problem of hunger can yield only to an increase in the productivity per acre and is virtually unaffected by increases in the productivity per man.

Let us then turn to our central question: how can the hungry countries learn to feed themselves? It is indeed a matter of learning. Of all the factors that serve to improve agriculture, unquestionably the most important is *method* – the methods of good husbandry. To talk only of better seeds and better stock, of a better 'infrastructure' in the shape of roads and other facilities, or of the injection of more capital, is in my opinion to miss the decisive factor. To go even further and suggest that the 'hunger gap' could be closed by industrial type farming with high mechanisation, chemical fertilisers, insecticides, and so forth, is to become dangerously misleading.

If there is an answer to the problem of hunger in the developing countries, it can be found only in the principles of good husbandry. The spectre of hunger arises because in chasing after the unattainable people fail to attend to that which is within their reach. Countries with surplus populations in the land, largely underemployed or even unemployed, allow themselves to be enticed into the adoption of farming methods which are suitable for the wide open spaces of underpopulated continents or for highly industrialised communities with a shortage of agricultural labour. Countries desperately short of capital mechanise agriculture, substituting capital for men, adding to unemployment, and reducing the yield per acre. In general, most types of high mechanisation and most chemicals used on the land are labour-saving devices and as such quite inappropriate for poor countries with a large unemployment problem. There are of course exceptions – which merely prove the rule. Some land, if it is to be ploughed at all, must be ploughed very quickly, which can only be done by mechanised means. Some soils suffer from certain pronounced chemical deficiencies and cannot grow any proper crop at all unless these deficiencies are made good. But these exceptions must not blind us to the fact that high mechanisation and the use of chemicals in agriculture are primarily labour-saving devices which can add to output only on the assumption that the labour otherwise needed could not be made available.

I am very much aware that these statements may strike many as highly controversial. Since chemical fertilisers are for the soil a stimulant, they often have a striking short-run effect, and since they cause something like an addiction, their withdrawal can produce a sharp drop of yields. But this proves nothing. Comparisons have to be made with non-addicted soils and over long periods. Where these have been made, the results speak for themselves. In every case it emerges that good husbandry, methodical working with the maximum use of farm wastes, etc., produces long-run results which are as good, if not better, than those produced with the help of chemicals. And much the same applies also to modern pesticides, weedkillers, and so forth, all of them, some special cases apart, labour-saving devices.

Where labour is the bottleneck, let us by all means apply labour-saving devices. But where labour is in surplus and industrial products are scarce, it is bad economics to substitute the latter for the former, and to do so means to divert attention from the one thing needful – honest, good husbandry.

We are talking about the developing countries, countries in the grip of poverty, containing about two-thirds of the world's population and growing fast. The total world production of artificial fertilisers in 1961-63 amounted to about 35 million tons a year of which only 1.8 million tons, or 5 percent was produced in the developing countries. The Food and Agriculture Organisation has calculated that these countries should use 19 million tons by 1970 and 35 million tons by 1980 – about thirteen years from now. I consider the attainment of such targets an absolute impossibility. But even if they could be attained, can millions, hundreds of millions of cultivators be taught to use them in a manner that does not hopelessly poison the soil? And if they can be taught, can they not equally, and probably more easily, be taught to adopt methods of good husbandry capable of achieving the same or even better results without artificial fertilisers? Experience shows that excellent farming with superlative yields per acre is possible and in fact being practiced by individual farmers all over the world, without recourse to these costly products of industry. Where the methods are good, the yields are high, and where the methods are poor, slovenly, and therefore wasteful, even artificial fertilisers do not produce good results. I wish the time would come when people would pay as much attention to a simple matter like farm accountancy in developing countries as they now devote to utopian dreams of educating a largely illiterate population in the intelligent use of dangerous materials like fertilisers, pesticides and so forth.

However that may be, one thing stands out: the hungry nations cannot get enough of these devices. They do not have the money to buy them and there is not enough aid available to let them have them free. It is no use telling them what they could do if they were already rich. A classic example of this kind of thinking can be found in the same issue of '*Time*' from which I have already quoted. I quote again:

> "If the short-range solution to hunger overseas is more United States food, the long-range answer must be the export of technology, along with capital and brains to see that it is applied wisely. The rest of the world needs to catch up with the mechanisation and efficiency of US farms. Half the world's tractors operate in North America. California rice growers have gone so far as to plant, fertilise and spray their crops entirely from planes. A single US farm worker now feeds 37 people."

One wonders to whom this advice is directed. To Japan, or Italy, or Egypt, or Spain, where rice yields per acre are substantially higher than they are in the United States? Or to India, Pakistan and others, where the rice grower's income is so pitiful that he could not afford a bicycle, let alone a plane? But let me continue to quote:

> "Vital as research is, victory over hunger also demands that backward countries scale new heights of social, political and economic organisation. As the US example shows, it takes vast amounts of capital – $30,500 per US farm worker vs. $19,600 for an industrial worker… With carrot and stick, the US now offers the underdeveloped world a chance – perhaps its last – to borrow US techniques and reach for the same nourishing reward."

You might think it a bit unfair of me to quote such absurdities. Unfortunately, they are not untypical of what many people, even in high places, are thinking, saying, and doing. Just think of it: thirty thousand dollars per farm worker in India or Nigeria – so that he will then be able to feed 37 people, who will thereupon, no doubt, migrate into the big towns where they will find workplaces costing twenty thousand dollars each. This is their 'last chance'. In India alone some 200 million such workplaces will be needed, and at an average of twenty-five thousand dollars a piece, this will cost the trifling sum of five thousand milliard dollars – roughly 10,000 times as much as the yearly aid India is currently receiving from the United States. Marie Antoinette acquired an unenviable reputation for asking, on a certain occasion: "Why do these people shout for bread? Why don't they eat cake?" In comparison with these modern pundits, she must rank as an eminently sensible woman.

No doubt the poor must be given help, but within the harsh framework set by their poverty. No doubt the poor need technological aid, but at a level that is appropriate to their actual conditions. The fundamental cause of hunger and misery in the developing countries, and particularly in South East Asia, is not their backwardness but the condition of decay into which they have fallen. Not being an historian I shall not attempt to analyse the historical causes. Today, the decay is there for all to see. We speak of decay when people are doing badly that which they used to do well. Decay is not overcome by enticing them to do something entirely different, which they will do even more badly. It is not a matter of rejecting anything that is good, and even the most modern, most highly industrialised, and most sophisticated farming methods may have their occasional applicability in developing countries (assuming these methods are really sound in themselves). But there is a time scale which must not be overlooked. If we are thinking of the next thirty years, the period during which, according to authoritative estimates, world food production must treble if widespread hunger is to be avoided, it is certain that these ultra-modern methods will be merely a fringe phenomenon in the developing countries and that the question of Hunger will continue to be decided by hundreds of millions of humble peasants working their land along traditional lines. It is *their* decay that has to be overcome: it is *their* methods that have to be in some way upgraded and rationalised: it is they who have to be given a chance of using their labour power more fully and to better purpose, both in agricultural pursuits. The only way to fight hunger in the hungry countries is to involve the entire rural population in a kind of agricultural renaissance, in a process of true growth in which education and economic development go hand in hand.

Assume for a moment some sort of world government had at its disposal some twenty-five milliard dollars a year of aid funds, that is, perhaps three times the amount of aid currently being made available. At $25,000 a workplace, this aid could purchase a million new workplaces a year, whether in agriculture or industry. But at $250 per workplace, one hundred million workplaces could be newly created or substantially upgraded, and then we would start talking sense. For this is the relevant order of magnitude: a hundred million, not one million. In discussing the problem of world hunger we must talk of things capable of affecting hundreds of millions of peasants, otherwise we are wasting our time.

If, therefore, the capital endowment per workplace is screwed up to the level of modern technology, even the biggest conceivable aid programmes will not really touch the masses of peasants, the custodians of the soil on whose efforts everything depends. It follows that the real question is this: how can workplaces be upgraded, or newly created, with a capital expenditure of, say, $250 per workplace?

The twenty-five thousand dollar technology of the rich countries is readily available for anyone who is already rich; it is totally out of reach and therefore totally irrelevant for the poor peasants of this world. A two hundred and fifty dollar technology would mean something to them – in the context of aid, and it could reach a sufficient number of them to matter. Such a technology, which I have named 'Intermediate Technology' would be immensely more productive and more viable than the decayed traditional technology of those countries. It would, moreover, have the right educational impact, which is essential, for unless education and economic development go together there can be no genuine development at all.

The appropriate Intermediate Technologies already exist all over the world, even in the most highly developed countries; but they exist in an obscure and scattered way, so that the people who need them cannot find them. The whole process of aid tends to bypass them; it tends to offer the poor – with carrot and stick, as *Time* put it – the tools of the rich, which means that the poor get nothing at all and those already rich – who also exist in the poor countries – grow even richer. Officials, of course, tend to favour the glamorous technology, which is photogenic and something to boast about and raises no awkward questions of how to obtain the active participation of millions of people. But the price of this preference is a heavy one: a lack of real development and the prospect of world hunger.

Think of it – that in this year 1966 the Food and Agriculture Organisation of the United Nations tells us that the food availability per head in the developing countries is no greater today than it was in the 1930's, that food output has barely kept pace with the growth of population. But in the process the number of destitute people has vastly increased, while a wealthy minority has profited. Can this be called development? Is this the outcome of aid? Is it conceivable that human nature in the developing countries is so inadequate that this meagre result would not have been obtained even in the absence of aid? Is it possible that the aid giving has been largely futile? I do not know. Much of the aid effort has certainly been misconceived, which is not surprising, considering how difficult it is for the rich to understand the conditions of the poor. It is a tragic story, because there has been no lack of goodwill and genuine concern.

However that may be, even if we cannot solve the psychological problems, we can inject some new thinking into the debate on World Hunger and Economic Development by insisting that the technologies offered to the poor must be appropriate to the actual conditions of poverty, if they are to be of help. They must be Intermediate Technologies.

To promote these ideas – and to do something towards their implementation – a private, non-profit organisation has recently been set up in London under the name of Intermediate Technology Development Group Limited[1]. One of the main purposes of the Group is to keep in intimate contact with industry, consulting engineers, and, of course, all aid giving agencies. The response from industry has been magnificent and that from the developing countries, overwhelming. In all matters the Group tries to develop the 'basic approach'. Its slogans are 'Tools for Progress' and 'Education for Self-Help'. Now, what is the basic approach in agriculture?

In many developing countries, the most basic agricultural problem is water. In the aid field, most of the thinking about water has been in terms of enormous dams and irrigation projects, costing millions of pounds. But the water is most needed exactly where it falls as rain, at the peasants doorstep. If the peasant has to trek many miles to reach water, his position remains one of unalterable misery. The real task is to catch the water where it falls, in rainwater catchment tanks so designed that water will remain cool and protected and will neither seep away nor evaporate under the hot sun. A suitable technique has been devised by Mr. Michael Ionides by brilliantly combining the most ancient technique of water conservation practiced in the Sudan, with modern knowledge and materials. The result is a method which exactly fits the conditions of poor villagers who lack purchasing power but have a fairly ample supply of local labour. Every village should now be able to obtain a protected water supply, mainly by applying their own labour power.

The proper method has thus been developed; but to make it really available to the poor and needy, who are counted in hundreds of millions, two further steps, in my opinion, have to be taken. The method needs to be reduced, as it were, to a do-it-yourself-kit, containing all required materials and the necessary instructions in a form which simple villagers can understand, and so proportioned that it easily fits on to a Land Rover. And there must be a big educational effort throughout the needy countries, using the existing primary school systems for the purpose. This would really be 'basic education', that is, an education designed to fit the pupil to live successfully in the actual conditions of his own country. It is only when these additional two steps are taken – two steps beyond the development of the method itself – that a real contribution to the problems of World Hunger and World Development will be made.

Let me give another example, very simple and down-to-earth. In many semi-arid regions the main occupation is cattle raising. The productivity – both per acre and per man – can be enormously increased by controlling grazing, which however normally requires extensive fencing. What is the cost of fencing in Africa? People open a drawer full of quotations from the developed countries, and the answer is "£100 a mile". At this cost, it is obvious, extensive fencing is utterly beyond the reach of poor villagers. This problem still awaits its Michael Ionides. I hope the Intermediate Technology Development Group will tackle it. We need a really low-cost method of fencing, with a maximum use of local labour and a minimum use of in-bought materials, and that method 'reduced' to a do-it-yourself-kit to fit on to a Land Rover. And then everybody who needs it must somehow be told about it and have a chance of acquiring the know-how.

Countless other examples could be given. High on the priority list must be the problem of crop storage. It is a matter of pretty well established fact that the poorest countries suffer the greatest losses – often thirty to forty percent of the harvest – because of lack of proper storage. Yet I doubt that there is an insufficiency of knowledge and experience on how to store safely. Only, the existing knowledge does not reach those who need it most; it has not been 'reduced' to a do-it-yourself-kit and has not been introduced into the primary school curriculum – if you will allow me this slightly symbolic way of expressing myself. The same basic approach has to be applied to every form of building, bridging, transport, and processing and other production in rural areas, with the invariable objective of minimising the need for in-bought materials and thus enabling the poor peasants to utilise their one major asset, their own labour power, but on a much higher level of productivity and viability than is common at present.

I believe that the problem of World Hunger can be solved along these lines and *along these lines only.* At the risk of repeating myself I emphasise that the poor peasants are the custodians of the soil in the hungry countries and that it is the poor peasants and no one else who will, or will not, double and treble the productivity of their acres, as is required if famine is to be avoided. Food is produced in rural areas, not in the big cities. Food surpluses from the rural areas are needed to feed the ever-growing cities. The central economic task of mankind, at this juncture, is to build up an efficient and satisfactory way of life in the rural areas, to achieve an agro-industrial structure which conquers unemployment, stops rural decay, and arrests the seemingly irresistible drift of destitute people from the countryside into the big cities, already overcrowded and rapidly becoming unmanageable.

The world food problem is not primarily a *scientific* problem. It is a problem of mass mobilisation, of mass education towards 'the next step', of making available the appropriate technologies to hundreds of millions of peasants. Needless to say, in many countries it is also a political problem – but this aspect goes beyond my present terms of reference.

It should be abundantly clear from what I have said that Factory Farming can have no relevance whatever to the question of avoiding famine in the hungry countries. What happens in the Factory Farms is not primary production, but secondary production: a process of conversion, like turning coal into electricity. No one, surely, makes the mistake of the dear old lady who after seeing a film about the tough life of coal miners exclaimed: "I shall never again burn coal, but immediately switch over to electricity!" When coal is burned to make electricity, about seventy percent of the calories contained in the coal are lost. When feeding stuffs are turned into poultry or veal in Factory Farms, some eighty to eighty-five percent of the calories contained in the feeding stuffs are lost. This conversion, therefore can have nothing to do with feeding the hungry.

It is also easy to see that the main *raison d'etre* of Factory Farming is to save human labour. Whether it ultimately achieves even this, may be doubtful; I am not qualified to judge it. What is certain is that the impulsion towards labour-saving does not reasonably exist in the hungry countries, which suffer from a surplus of labour and a shortage of capital.

A final point about Factory Farming in the developing countries is worth making. Perhaps the greatest problem of these countries is the problem of alienation, of being faced with so much that is strange and incomprehensible and incompatible with tradition that the ordinary people become bewildered and timid, while the educated lose contact with the ordinary people. And what more terrible method of alienation could be devised than a type of farming that alienated even the animals from their natural life and induced man to treat them in a manner utterly irreconcilable with the simplest teachings of religion?

For a man to put himself into a wrongful relationship with animals and particularly those long domesticated by him, has always been considered a horrible and infinitely dangerous thing to do. There have been no holy men in our history or in anybody else's history who were cruel to animals, and innumerable are the stories and legends which link sanctity with a loving kindness towards lower creation. In *Proverbs* we read that the just man takes care of his beast, but the heart of the wicked is merciless, and St. Thomas Aquinas wrote: "It is evident that if a man practices a compassionate affection for animals, he is all the more disposed to feel compassion for his fellow men." And I might also quote Pope Pius XII who said: "The animal world, as all creation, is a manifestation of God's power, his wisdom, and his goodness, and as such deserves man's respect and consideration. Any reckless desire to kill off animals, all unnecessary harshness and callous cruelty toward them is to be condemned. Such conduct, moreover, is baneful to a healthy human sentiment and only tends to brutalise it".

Have the sayings of the saints and sages anything to do with the practical problem of feeding the hungry? Yes. Man does not live by bread alone and if he thinks he can disregard this truth and can allow the 'human sentiment' to become brutalised, he does not lose his technical intelligence but his power of sound judgement, with the result that even the bread fails him – in one way or another. Another way of putting the same thing is this: man's greatest single task today is to develop in himself the power of non-violence. Everything he does violently, for instance in agriculture, could also be done relatively non-violently, that is, gently, organically, patiently adapted to the rhythms of life. The true task of all further research and development is surely to devise non-violent methods of reaching the results which man requires for his existence on earth. The violent methods always seem to produce bigger results more quickly; in fact, they lead to the accumulation of insoluble problems, particularly with the World Food Problem. But there is a way, a non-violent way. It is based on a true compassion for hundreds of millions of humble peasants throughout the world and an effort of the imagination to recognise the boundaries of their poverty. It leads to policies that truly help them to help themselves. This is the way we must seek. It is humane, democratic and, I can assure you, surprisingly cheap.

[1] The Centre is now located at: Schumacher Centre, Bourton Hall, Bourton on Dunsmore, Rugby CV23 9QZ

Chapter Three

The New Radicalism

Leopold Kohr

The question has frequently been asked: Is radicalism dead? With the advent of the affluent society, which the Labour Party's socialist reforms did so much to usher in, have not all its aims been fulfilled? What can Labour still be radical about?

Before one can answer the question, it is necessary to have a clear picture of what radicalism really means. Obviously it is an ideology urging change. But this would turn everybody into a radical. For who does not want change ? Life itself is change –the change of seasons, of growth, of ageing, of generations. What characterises a radical is that he desires change at an accelerated pace. Hence the first criterion concerns a question of mood, of temperament. A radical is impatient. He wants change fast.

But so does a criminal anxious to kill a person long before his time is up; does this make him a radical too ? There are quite a few who think so, and therefore reject all radicalism on grounds of temperament alone. But temperament alone is not the only element defining an ideology. It is also the purpose that counts. And the purpose of radicalism is not just to bring about change fast, but to do so in order to improve the human lot. The emphasis is on the human, not the social, lot. Considering society's practically indefinite span of life, no speed is needed to improve the *social* condition. Time's process of evolution will take care of this in the same way as it has taken care of the condition of ant and bee societies whose present stage of social perfection it accomplished without the need of radical assistance. But it is different with the *human* condition whose improvement must be accomplished within the brief span of life available to the individual. While society can thus wait, its citizens cannot. It is because of the latter that impatience and speed are both necessary and justified!

This gives us two defining elements of radicalism: impatient temperament, and a purpose benefiting the human person. But while this excludes the criminal, it would qualify the Archbishop of Canterbury as a radical – a high minded reformer anxious both to improve the lot of individual man, and to achieve the results fast enough to improve his condition as long as he is still alive. Yet we know that the venerable clergyman does not quite fit our image of a radical. A third defining element is therefore necessary. The non-radical reformer is continuously hampered by institutions which, owing their origin in an outmoded social environment, have long frozen all human relationships into patterns of customs and law which resist change not because of conservative tradition or evil intent but because of the rigidities inherent in the structure of every established order. Yet, the non-radical accepts all this because of his fondness for ancient trimmings to which he sees no other alternative. The radical, on the other hand, does not accept it. In his effort to overcome the delaying effect of existing institutions, he feels he must step outside the established order. He becomes a revolutionary.

With this we have the three essential ingredients that go into the make-up of a radical. His temperament is impatient for change. His purpose is the improvement of the lot of individual man. His method is revolution – the attempt to accomplish his purpose through the use of tools beyond the reach of the established system. It is this last criterion that distinguishes him from the well-meaning Archbishop who, though equally impatient for improving the human condition, tries to achieve it *within* the existing system.

But what distinguishes him from a fascist or a communist? Each of the two latter is impatient for change, and each aims at bringing about this change by stepping outside the established order, through revolution. Nevertheless they too fail to qualify as true radicals. For though they fulfil the requirements of the first and third criterion, they fall short in the case of the second. They want improvement, but not of man. Their concern belongs to society as a whole. In the interest of improving the stock, health, race, status, productivity and power of an organism whose longevity makes it practically imperishable anyway, they may sacrifice the short-lived human being by the millions.

Rather than being the beneficiary, the individual citizen becomes the victim of their grand design, undertaken for the glory of a future he will not live to enjoy, and as oppressive in its effect on the living as a prince building pyramids and palaces. If he ventures to make reference to his own purposes, he is called a traitor and liquidated.

This is why neither fascists nor communists, neither Castros nor Francos, though revolutionaries and reformers both, are true radicals. They hurry where there is no need to hurry.

They reform, but the wrong condition. This does not mean that the radical is insensitive to social reform. On the contrary. But he considers it the means, not the end of his aims. His end is the improvement not of the social but the human lot. The only question still to be answered is: what is exactly meant by improving the human lot?

Since the beginning of time, man's full enjoyment of life has been jeopardised by one principal condition: lack of freedom. This means that improvement as applied to the human lot can have only one meaning: liberation. The true radical is therefore a liberator. His purpose is to bring freedom to the individual. He is not interested in a *free society*. The most tyrannical societies are free. For this reason, the freedom of society may often be the very cause keeping the individual in subjection. Rome was free society. No other society could impose its will on it. But what good did it do to Cicero whose life it demanded as a sacrifice to its appetites? In our own time Switzerland is a free society in the sense that it has no sovereign above itself. But this of course also makes the Soviet Union a free society, or Communist China, or Nazi Germany, or Trujillo's Dominican Republic, Castro's Cuba, Franco's Spain, Tito's Yugoslavia. What the radical is interested in is a *society of the free* – a vastly different proposition. Improvement in the radical sense means therefore not improvement in diet, health or life expectancy. Every tyrant wants this for his soldiers; every exploiter for his workers. It means liberation – liberation from servitude; liberation from tyranny, including the tyranny emanating from society itself. A radical can be anti-social. He can never be anti-human.

Since there are four types of circumstances capable of depriving the individual of his freedom, radicalism has in the course of history produced not one but four movements of liberation. The first and most ancient was directed against religious superstition. The earliest radicals were therefore religious liberators. Fiercely resisted by the established order of priests, priest-kings, and god-kings, whose sinister power as sole interpreters of the divine will they had to break before they could liberate man from his terror of supernatural influences, each of them – Socrates, Christ, the Apostles – had to step outside the existing religious framework. Each was a revolutionary. And the freedom they brought was the first of the great freedoms that have helped man to realise his humanity; the freedom of mind, the freedom of conscience, the freedom to have his own identity, to be himself. Indeed by prying him loose from the collective haze of his superstitious group in which he had up till then been submerged like a diffuse image in a block of marble before the arrival of the sculptor, the religious liberators not only freed but created the individual. From now on his soul was his own, and God was in him, not in priest, king, or society.

However, having become conscious of himself, man soon began to realise that, though his mind had been set free, his person had not. He was a slave, a serf, a subordinate, human as any other but without status, without equality, without full dignity. The circumstance whose oppression he now felt most was no longer his religious but his political environment. The new representatives of radicalism, frequently evolving out of religious radicalism, were therefore the political liberators. From the Gracchi of ancient Rome to the Wilhelm Tells of the Middle Ages and the Liberals of 19th Century England, they had as their object the dignity of full citizenship and political equality for all. To the freedom of the mind they wanted to add the freedom of the human person. And again they had to step outside the existing order committed as it was to hierarchy and privilege. To accomplish their aims, they replaced aristocracy with democracy, monarchy with republic, or absolute monarchy with constitutional monarchy. The change of system was not always violent. But it was always fundamental and revolutionary.

As spiritual liberation resulted in the quest for political freedom, political liberation now led to the quest for economic freedom. For without the latter, the former would have remained a vain achievement. The seemingly last mission of radicalism was thus the economic liberation of man. Again the main obstacle lay in the existing order, this time capitalism which, though it had proved itself eminently capable of producing in abundance the goods necessary to insure a good life for all, seemed hopelessly at a loss when it came to distributing them in an equitable manner. The economic radicals therefore felt that they, too, must step outside the established system if they were to achieve the rapid pace of improvement they desired. The new system they introduced was socialism. Transferring the central power of production from the individual to the state, it now became possible to re-transfer an increased power of consumption from the state to the individual, thereby liquidating the last of the circumstances obstructing the happiness of the individual – the fear and tyranny of poverty.

With this all seems to have been accomplished. Religious radicalism had liberated man's mind through the establishment of modern faiths such as Islam, Judaism or Christianity, which should not be confused with the political organisation of these faiths in the form of church, mosque, or synagogue. Political radicalism had liberated his person by introducing representative liberal democracy. Economic radicalism has liberated his body through the establishment of the socialist welfare state. Now the age of affluence has set in. As a result, the question posed at the beginning seems indeed legitimate: Is socialism a spent force? And more than that: Is radicalism itself dead? Is there anything left that it could still achieve? Switch over from the improvement of the human to that of the social lot? And, in the process, re-enslave man in the grand manner of Egyptian kings? With the difference perhaps of putting us to work on traffic circles instead of Sphinxes? Or sputniks instead of pyramids? And making us lay down our lives for the glory of the state or the improvement of future generations who will bear us no more gratitude than we hold for the past, and who will justly admire no one except the society-reforming monster who managed to extract our purposeless sacrifice ?

Actually, however, there is a fourth circumstance threatening the freedom of the individual, a fourth freedom to be secured, and hence a fourth type of radicalism. And it is this, not liberalism or socialism, that is beginning to fight the battle for freedom in our age. Unlike the others, the fourth threat to freedom has inadvertently but inescapably emerged as a by-product of the liberation from the third. For in order to fulfil its mission of freeing man from the iniquities of capitalist distribution, socialism had to increase first the scope, then the function, and finally the power of the state. And it is the power of the state that constitutes both the newest and the most terrible threat to freedom. For as this power increases, the danger rises that the tool of the citizen's welfare becomes the master of the citizen; and the pluralist state in which the individual is sovereign becomes the Unitarian state in which the state is sovereign; that the society of the free turns into the meaningless self-glorifying concept of the free society of 1984. Though up to a certain point the interests of the two are complementary, they become mutually exclusive when the power of the state assumes such proportions that its sheer weight begins to obliterate the freedom-serving institutions which it had previously provided.

The fourth and last form of radicalism is therefore no longer directed against capitalist exploitation, political privilege or religious superstition. Socialists, Liberals, and Christians have taken care of these. It is directed against the power of the state, symbolised by the swollen sponge of Parkinsonian bureaucracy. Since this is proportionate to the size of society on which it feeds, it follows that the most modern form of radicalism, having again to step outside the existing order to accomplish its ends, must aim at centering social life in national communities whose size is so reduced as to render excessive governmental power both impossible and unnecessary. For what good is the welfare state if its costs of administration become larger than the benefits it yields ?

The new radicals are therefore the decentralisers, the federalisers, the regionalists, the regional nationalists (in contrast to the centralising, expansionist and hence non-radical nationalistic power megalomaniacs) such as they begin to emerge in all corners of the world. We need only to think of the old movements in such traditionally radical communities as Sicily, Catalonia, Brittany, Scotland, Wales, or of such newer ones as they have recently appeared in Naga, Quebec, Tibet, Goa, Somalia and elsewhere.

The freedom they offer to ensure the trinity of the other freedoms is the freedom from government, not in the economic sense of *laissez faire* but in a personal sense. As Gwynfor Evans, one of the most inspiring representatives of this new radicalism fighting to protect the individual from the tyranny of government, writes so succinctly in his programme for an independent Wales:

> "The decentralist would limit the power of the State... In a total-itarian order even the nation may be swallowed by the State, and this complete inversion of the right order has not been uncommon in our time. Still more often, in countries not rigidly totalitarian, we see within the nation religious, social and economic communities being weakened or destroyed by State action. This is a very grave loss, for these communities do much to develop man's personality and to provide bulwarks against the State's erosion of individual freedom. The individual person must therefore be enabled to withstand the State when it over-reaches itself... In the Welsh nationalist view therefore the nation is a community of communities, and the State fails in its proper function if these communities are weakened rather than strength-ened by it."

Thus while socialist radicalism may indeed have fulfilled its mission, radicalism itself is far from being dead. Its fourth man-ifestation is only just beginning.

Chapter Four

Buddhist Economics

E. F. Schumacher

'Right Livelihood' is one of the requirements of the Buddha's Noble Eightfold Path. It is clear, therefore, that there must be such a thing as Buddhist Economics.

Buddhist countries, at the same time, have often stated that they wish to remain faithful to their heritage. So Burma: "The New Burma sees no conflict between religious values and economic process. Spiritual health and material well-being are not enemies: they are natural allies." Or: "We can blend successfully the religious and spiritual values of our heritage with the benefits of modern technology." Or: "We Burmans have a sacred duty to conform both our dreams and our acts to our faith. This we shall ever do."

All the same, such countries invariably assume that they can model their economic development plans in accordance with modern economics, and they call upon modern economists from so-called advanced countries to advise them, to formulate the policies to be pursued, and to construct the grand design for development, the Five-Year Plan or whatever it may be called. No one seems to think that a Buddhist way of life would call for Buddhist economics, just as the modern materialist way of life has brought forth modern economics.

Economists themselves, like most specialists, normally suffer from a kind of metaphysical blindness, assuming that theirs is a science of absolute and invariable truths, without any pre-suppositions. Some go as far as to claim that economic laws are as free from 'metaphysics' or 'values' as the law of gravitation. We need not, however, get involved in arguments of methodology. Instead, let us take some fundamentals and see what they look like when viewed by a modern economist and a Buddhist economist.

There is universal agreement that the fundamental source of wealth is human labour. Now, the modern economist has been brought up to consider 'labour' or work as little more than a necessary evil. From the point of view of the employer, it is in any case simply an item of cost, to be reduced to a minimum if it cannot be eliminated altogether, say, by automation. From the point of view of the workman, it is a 'disutility'; to work is to make a sacrifice of one's leisure and comfort, and wages are a kind of compensation for the sacrifice. Hence the ideal from the point of view of the employer is to have output without employees, and the ideal from the point of view of the employee is to have income without employment.

The consequences of these attitudes both in theory and in practice are, of course, extremely far-reaching. If the ideal with regard to work is to get rid of it, every method that 'reduces the work load' is a good thing. The most potent method, short of automation, is the so-called 'division of labour' and the classical example is the pin factory eulogised in Adam Smith's *Wealth of Nations*. Here it is not a matter of ordinary specialisation, which mankind has practised from time immemorial, but of dividing up every complete process of production into minute parts, so that the final product can be produced at great speed without anyone having had to contribute more than a totally insignificant and, in most cases, unskilled movement of his limbs.

WORK

The Buddhist point of view takes the function of work to be at least threefold: to give a man a chance to utilise and develop his faculties; to enable him to overcome his ego-centeredness by joining with other people in a common task; and to bring forth the goods and services needed for a becoming existence. Again, the consequences that flow from this view are endless. To organise work in such a manner that it becomes meaningless, boring, stultifying, or nerve-racking for the worker would be little short of criminal; it would indicate a greater concern with goods than with people, an evil lack of compassion and a soul-destroying degree of attachment to the most primitive side of this worldly existence. Equally, to strive for leisure as an alternative to work would be considered a complete misunderstanding of one of the basic truths of human existence, namely, that work and leisure are complementary parts of the same living process and cannot be separated without destroying the joy of work and the bliss of leisure.

From the Buddhist point of view, there are therefore two types of mechanisation which must be clearly distinguished: one that enhances a man's skill and power and one that turns the work of man over to a mechanical slave, leaving man in a position of having to serve the slave. How to tell the one from the other? "The craftsman himself", says Ananda Coomaraswamy, a man equally competent to talk about the Modern West as the Ancient East, "the craftsman himself can always, if allowed to, draw the delicate distinction between the machine and the tool. The carpet loom is a tool, a contrivance for holding warp threads at a stretch for the pile to be woven round them by the craftsmen's fingers; but the power loom is a machine, and its significance as a destroyer of culture lies in the fact that it does the essentially human part of the work". It is clear, therefore, that Buddhist economics must be very different from the economics of modern materialism, since the Buddhist sees the essence of civilisation not in a multiplication of wants but in the purification of human character. Character, at the same time, is formed primarily by a man's work. And work, properly conducted in conditions of human dignity and freedom, blesses those who do it and equally their products. The Indian philosopher and economist J. C. Kumarappa sums the matter up as follows:

> "If the nature of the work is properly appreciated and applied, it will stand in the same relation to the higher faculties as food is to the physical body. It nourishes and enlivens the higher man and urges him to produce the best he is capable of. It directs his freewill along the proper course and disciplines the animal in him into progressive channels. It furnishes an excellent background for man to display his scale of values and develop his personality."

If a man has no chance of obtaining work he is in a desperate position, not simply because he lacks an income but because he lacks this nourishing and enlivening factor of disciplined work which nothing can replace. A modern economist may engage in highly sophisticated calculations on whether full employment 'pays' or whether it might be more 'economic' to run an economy at less than full employment so as to ensure a greater mobility of labour, a better stability of wages, and so forth. His fundamental criterion of success is simply the total quantity of goods produced during a given period of time. "If the marginal urgency of goods is low", says Professor Galbraith in *The Affluent Society*, "then so is the urgency of employing the last man or the last million men in the labour force." And again: "If … we can afford some unemployment in the interest of stability – a proposition, incidentally, of impeccably conservative antecedents – then we can afford to give those who are unemployed the goods that enable them to sustain their accustomed standard of living."

From a Buddhist point of view, this is standing the truth on its head by considering goods as more important than creative activity. It means shifting the emphasis from the worker to the product of work, that is, from the human to the sub-human, a surrender to the forces of evil. The very start of Buddhist economic planning would be a planning for full employment, and the primary purpose of this would in fact be employment for everyone who needs an 'outside' job: it would not be the maximisation of employment nor the maximisation of production. Women, on the whole, do not need an 'outside' job, and the large-scale employment of women in offices or factories would be considered a sign of serious economic failure. In particular, to let mothers of young children work in factories while the children run wild would be as uneconomic as the employment of a skilled worker as a soldier in the eyes of a modern economist.

While the materialist is mainly interested in goods, the Buddhist is mainly interested in liberation. But Buddhism is 'The Middle Way' and therefore in no way antagonistic to physical well-being. It is not wealth that stands in the way of liberation but the attachment to wealth; not the enjoyment of pleasurable things but the craving for them. The keynote of Buddhist economics, therefore, is simplicity and non-violence. From an economist's point of view, the marvel of the Buddhist way of life is the utter rationality of its pattern – amazingly small means leading to extraordinary satisfactory results.

STANDARD OF LIVING

For the modern economist this is very difficult to understand. He is used to measuring the 'standard of living' by the amount of annual consumption, assuming all the time that a man who consumes more is 'better off' than a man who consumes less. A Buddhist economist would consider this approach excessively irrational: since consumption is merely a means to human well-being, the aim should be to obtain the maximum of well-being with the minimum of consumption. Thus, if the purpose of clothing is a certain amount of temperature comfort and an attractive appearance, the task is to attain this purpose with the smallest possible effort, that is, with the smallest annual destruction of cloth and with the help of designs that involve the smallest possible input of toil. The less toil there is, the more time and strength is left for artistic creativity. It would be highly uneconomic, for instance, to go in for complicated tailoring, like the modern West, when a much more beautiful effect can be achieved by the skilful draping of uncut material. It would be the height of folly to make material so that it should wear out quickly and the height of barbarity to make anything ugly, shabby or mean. What has just been said about clothing applies equally to all other human requirements. The ownership and the consumption of goods is a means to an end, and Buddhist economics is the systematic study of how to attain given ends within the minimum means.

Modern economics, on the other hand, considers consumption to be the sole end and purpose of all economic activity, taking the factors of production – land, labour and capital – as the means. The former, in short, tries to maximise human satisfactions by the optimal pattern of consumption, while the latter tries to maximise consumption by the optimal pattern of productive effort. It is easy to see that the effort needed to sustain a way of life which seeks to obtain the optimal pattern consumption is likely to be much smaller than the effort need to sustain a drive for maximum consumption. We need not be surprised, therefore, that the pressure and strain of living is very much less in, say, Burma than it is in the United States, in spite of the fact that the amount of labour-saving machinery used in the former country is only a minute fraction of the amount used in the latter.

PATTERN OF CONSUMPTION

Simplicity and non-violence are obviously closely related. The optimal pattern of consumption, producing a high degree of human satisfaction by means of a relatively low rate of consumption, allows people to live without great pressure and strain and to fulfil the primary injunction of Buddhist teaching: 'Cease to do evil; try to do good.' As physical resources are everywhere limited, people satisfying their needs by means of a modest use of resources are obviously less likely to be at each other's throats than people depending upon a high rate of use. Equally, people who live in highly self-sufficient local communities are less likely to get involved in large-scale violence than people whose existence depends on world-wide systems of trade.

From the point of view of Buddhist economics, therefore, production from local resources for local needs is the most rational way of economic life, while dependence on imports from afar and the consequent need to produce for export to unknown and distant peoples is highly uneconomic and justifiable only in exceptional cases and on a small scale. Just as the modern economist would admit that a high rate of consumption of transport services between a man's home and his place of work signifies a misfortune and not a high standard of life, so the Buddhist economist would hold that to satisfy human wants from far-away sources rather than from sources nearby signifies failure rather than success. The former might take statistics showing an increase in the number of ton/miles per head of the population carried by a country's transport system as proof of economic progress, while to the latter – the Buddhist economist – the same statistics would indicate a highly undesirable deterioration in the *pattern* of consumption.

NATURAL RESOURCES

Another striking difference between modern economics and Buddhist economics arises over the use of natural resources. Bertrand de Juvenal, the eminent French political philosopher, has characterised 'Western man' in words which may be taken as a fair description of the modern economist:

"He tends to count nothing as an expenditure, other than human effort; he does not seem to mind how much mineral matter he wastes and, far worse, how much living matter he destroys. He does not seem to realise at all that human life is a dependent part of an ecosystem of many different forms of life. As the world is ruled from towns where men are cut off from any form of life other than human, the feeling of belonging to an ecosystem is not revived. This results in a harsh and improvident treatment of things upon which we ultimately depend, such as water and trees."

The teaching of the Buddha, on the other hand, enjoins a reverent and non-violent attitude not only to all sentient beings but also, with great emphasis, to trees. Every follower of the Buddha ought to plant a tree every few years and look after it until it is safely established, and the Buddhist economist can demonstrate without difficulty that the universal observance of this rule would result in a high rate of genuine economic development independent of any foreign aid. Much of the economic decay of South-East Asia (as of many other parts of the world) is undoubtedly due to a heedless and shameful neglect of trees.

Modern economics does not distinguish between renewable and non-renewable materials, as its very method is to equalise and quantify everything by means of a money price. Thus, taking various alternative fuels, like coal, oil, wood or water power: the only difference between them recognised by modern economics is relative cost per equivalent unit. The cheapest is automatically the one to be preferred, as to do otherwise would be irrational and 'uneconomic'. From a Buddhist point of view, of course, this will not do; the essential difference between non-renewable fuels like coal and oil on the one hand and renewable fuels like wood and water-power on the other cannot be simply over-looked. Non-renewable goods must be used only if they are indispensable, and then only with the greatest care and the most meticulous concern for conservation. To use them heedlessly or extravagantly is an act of violence, and while complete non-violence may not be attainable on this earth, there is none the less an ineluctable duty on man to aim at the ideal of non-violence in all he does.

Just as a modern European economist would not consider it a great economic achievement if all European art treasures were sold to America at attractive prices, so the Buddhist economist would insist that a population basing its economic life on non-renewable fuels is living parasitically, on capital instead of income. Such a way of life could have no permanence and could therefore be justified only as a purely temporary expedient. As the world's resources of non-renewable fuels – coal, oil and natural gas – are exceedingly unevenly distributed over the globe and undoubtedly limited in quantity, it is clear that their exploitation at an ever increasing rate is an act of violence against nature which must almost inevitably lead to violence between men.

The Middle Way

This fact alone might give food for thought even to those people in Buddhist countries who care nothing for the religious and spiritual values of their heritage and ardently desire to embrace the materialism of modern economics at the fastest possible speed. Before they dismiss Buddhist economics as nothing better than a nostalgic dream, they might wish to consider whether the path of economic development outlined by modern economics is likely to lead them to places where they really want to be. Towards the end of his courageous book *The Challenge of Man's Future*, Professor Harrison Brown of the California Institute of Technology gives the following appraisal:

"Thus we see that, just as industrial society is fundamentally unstable and subject to reversion to agrarian existence, so within it the conditions which offer individual freedom are unstable in their ability to avoid the conditions which impose rigid organisation and totalitarian control. Indeed, when we examine all of the foreseeable difficulties which threaten the survival of industrial civilisation, it is difficult to see how the achievement of stability and the maintenance of individual liberty can be made compatible."

Even if this were dismissed as a long-term view – and in the long term, as Keynes said, we are all dead – there is the immediate question of whether 'modernisation', as currently practised without regard to religious and spiritual values, is actually producing agreeable results. As far as the masses are concerned, the results appear to be disastrous – a collapse of the rural economy, a rising tide of unemployment in town and country, and the growth of a city proletariat without nourishment for either body or soul.

It is in the light of both immediate experience and long-term prospects that the study of Buddhist economics could be recommended even to those who believe that economic growth is more important than any spiritual or religious values. For it is not a question of choosing between 'modern growth' and 'traditional stagnation'. It is a question of finding the right path of development, the Middle Way between materialist heedlessness and traditionalist immobility, in short, of finding 'Right Livelihood'.

That this can be done is not in doubt. But it requires much more than blind imitation of the materialist way of life of the so-called advanced countries. It requires above all, 'the conscious and systematic development of a Middle Way in technology', as I have called it, a technology more productive and powerful than the decayed technology of the ancient East, but a the same time non-violent and immensely cheaper and simpler than the labour-saving technology of the modern West.

Chapter Five

Size Cycles

Leopold Kohr

The reason why, aside from the Russians, who predicted them for the wrong reasons, the post-war recessions of the Western world have been foreseen by so few is that a new type of cyclical fluctuation has made its appearance of which economic theory has not yet taken proper notice.

Fluctuations in the nineteenth-century and up to the second decade of the twentieth, were mainly in the nature of old-fashioned business cycles, they were the price that had to be paid for the enjoyment of an uncontrolled free-enterprise system. Only the setting up of government controls could avert their increasingly painful effects. Under the guiding influence of John Maynard Keynes, such controls have since been accepted in most capitalist countries, diminishing their freedom but saving them from the mounting severity of their depressions.

Yet, after 25 years of experimentation with government controls, recessions began to reappear and, as previously, to grow in intensity with repetition. Keynes himself may have anticipated this when he wrote in the 1930s that by 1955 most Treasuries of the world would have adopted his theories; but by then they would be not only obsolete but dangerous. Since policies based on his theories have failed to prevent the more recent recessions, both his foresight and his gloom seem to have been borne out.

The reason for this lies in a delayed secondary effect of government control which, though predictable, has never really been examined. The impact effect was invariably the seeming elimination of cycles – seeming because the cyclical forces pressing downward were not abolished but merely held in check by compensatory government action each time they threatened to assert themselves. In other words, visible cycles were turned into hidden cycles. This would have been good enough had not the government-induced absence of downswings caused such unprecedented economic growth that it actually magnified along with the forces pushing up also those pressing down. Ultimately, a point had to be reached as a result of the disproportionately increasing scale of economic activities, at which no measure of *added* control could cope with a situation that had begun to *outgrow* all human control.

For effective control requires either perfect visibility or a safety margin wide enough to be able to absorb the consequences of human error and miscalculation without distorting the anticipated results. But neither is possible in economies whose scale has become excessively large. The first, because what is too large cannot be perfectly visible. The second, because mass production, over-expansion, and the pressure of giant economic forces so reduce the all-determining margin between profit and cost that the minutest miscalculation may not only produce results diametrically opposite to those to which plans have been adjusted, but as in the case of shots to Mars, a minor error may push them so far in either direction that even powerful government intervention may become useless. For what applies to the multiplier that magnifies even minor miscalculations on the part of business, applies even more to miscalculations affecting the massive government-inspired measures designed to correct them. This is why the tight money policy instituted (prior to the famously unpredicted 1957 recession in the United States) in order to prevent the economy from taking off too high into space, was in retrospect considered by many economists as one of the very causes which subsequently pushed it too close to the ground. Instead of ending a crisis, controlled intervention merely produced a different sort of crisis which in this particular instance was given the ingenious name of *disinflation*.

The reason for the increasing failure of the governmental control mechanism is that from the end of the second world war onwards a previously unobserved new phenomenon has made its appearance, suggesting that the most recent fluctuations are no longer caused by any particular *system* but by the *scale* which modern economic activities have assumed. Capitalism no longer figures. Like waves in the ocean, these giant economic swells are caused by the chain-reacting instability inherent in everything that has grown too large, be it a heavy atom, a building, a market, or a state. They are no longer *business*, but what may be called, scale or *size cycles* which take their amplitude not from any particular economic system but from the size of the body politic through which they pass. Unlike the old-fashioned business cycles, size cycles are therefore not diminished but magnified by the economic integrating and expanding effect produced by government controls. This is why, to the puzzlement of communist and capitalist observers alike, they have made their appearance even in such a tightly controlled but equally overgrown economy as that of the Soviet Union which, being Socialist, should according to Marxist theory not have been subject to economic fluctuations such as characterise uncontrolled free-enterprise systems in the first place. Yet it was.

Now if the true problem of our age lies in size rather than in business cycles, it follows that what must be done is not to increase government controls until they match the devastating scale of the new type of economic fluctuations; nor will their dismantlement produce any results; what must be done is to reduce the size of the body politic, which gives them their devastating scale, until they become once again a match for the limited talent available to the ordinary mortals of which governments are composed.

In other words instead of centralisation let us have economic cantonisation. Let us replace the oceanic dimensions of integrated big powers and common markets by a devolved dyke system of inter-connected but highly self-sufficient local markets and mall states in which economic fluctuations can be controlled not because our leaders have Yale degrees, but because the ripples of a pond, however animated, can never assume the scale of the huge swells passing through the united water masses of the open seas. Then will not only controls be effective, as Keynes proposed, but also a system without controls such as Mrs Thatcher and Ronald Reagan would like to install.

Chapter Six

Healthy Development

E. F. Schumacher

By way of introduction, a short report from East Africa:

The Dutch manager of the textile plant received me with the greatest courtesy and not at all with the suspicion and irritated resentment I had half expected. "Another official visitor", he might well have thought, "to steal my time and ask more or less irrelevant questions". And, of course, I was going to ask plenty of questions.

"This plant, as you will see, is highly automated", he said.

"Before you go on", I interrupted, "could you just explain one thing to me. As I was coming in I noticed some hundred or so young African men at the factory gates, and armed guards keeping them out. Is this a riot or something?"

The Dutchman laughed: "Oh no! They are always there. They hope that I might sack someone and that they could step into his job".

"So you have quite a bit of unemployment in this town?"

"Yes, terrible".

"Thank you; excuse the interruption. Please carry on".

"This plant, as you will see", said the Dutchman, "is one of the most modern in East Africa, highly automated. We employ about 500 people, but this is much too much. We hope to get the number down quite considerably as our automated equipment becomes fully operative".

"So there is not much hope for the chaps outside?"

"No, I am afraid, there isn't".

"Tell me, what would be the total capital value of a plant like this?"

"About £1½ million".

"For 500 jobs", I calculated aloud, "this means about £3,000 per workplace. That's a lot of money for a poor country, the sort of 'capital intensity' we have in Western Europe or the United States".

"Yes indeed", said my Dutch friend, "my plant is as modern as you would find anywhere in the world".

He must have noticed my astonishment.

"You see", he continued, "we have to be competitive. The quality demanded today is very high. I cannot afford to send out faulty material. It is terribly difficult to train these people here to work faultlessly; they have no tradition of industrial discipline. Machines make no mistakes; human beings do. To get a high quality product we must eliminate the human factor".

"I quite understand", I said, "but tell me this: why has this factory been placed in this small town? Surely, you would be better off, marketwise and in every other respect, in the capital city?"

"Indeed we would. We did not want to come here. This was a planning decision of the Government".

"What was their reasoning?"

"Very simple", he said. "There is a lot of unemployment in this region. So we had to come here".

"I see. And your aim is to eliminate the human factor?"

"Yes", said the Dutchman. "I can see there is a conflict here. But I have to make this investment pay. What can I do?"

The problem is two-fold; how to obtain faster development and how to obtain healthy development. On a superficial view, the two parts of the problem are in conflict; on a deeper view, they are complementary, except in the very short term.

Evidence of unhealthy development exists all over the world, including some of the richest countries. It leads to a degradation of people and a ruination of the environment. Development is healthy only if it leads to an upgrading of people on the widest possible scale and an upgrading of their environment also on the widest possible scale.

What is the main cause of 'development' going wrong? It is the neglect of the geographical (locational) factor. While all development work is difficult, it is much easier in the big city – normally the capital city – than in the secondary towns; in the bigger towns, than in the little towns; and it is most difficult in the rural areas.

The free play of economic forces invariably favours the urban as against the rural areas, the big towns as against the small. It tends to produce the triple disease of mass migration into cities, mass unemployment, and the danger of famine.

Mushrooming cities, surrounded by ever-growing misery-belts, infested by a largely unemployed proletariat without nourishment for body or soul, can be found all over the world. For a rich minority, they offer the high life of extravagant luxury, albeit under the shadow of personal insecurity owing to the prevalence of crime and the symptoms of political instability. For the destitute majority they offer nothing but degradation. The rural areas, meanwhile, tend to sink into ever deeper decay. Every gifted person tries to migrate into the city, to escape from rural misery, and this irresistible 'brain drain' makes the problems of the rural hinterland ever more intractable. At the end of this kind of 'development' lies social chaos, the degradation of man and of his environment.

Most developing countries are overwhelmingly agricultural and must obviously give primary emphasis and attention to the development and upgrading of their agriculture. As agriculture cannot be practised in towns, it is the rural areas that must receive the main emphasis and attention.

What kind of emphasis and attention? It is of little use to go to semi-literate peasants engaged in primitive subsistence farming and expect them to adopt and successfully to practise modern farming methods. Poverty is a vicious circle; it feeds upon itself. The vicious circle of rural poverty can be broken only by introducing non-agricultural activities in the rural areas. These activities may be summed up in two words: industry and culture.

Agriculture alone, at the level of poverty, consisting as it does of scraping the ground and living with cattle, cannot develop the mind. Agricultural populations need the stimulus of non-agricultural activities, or they will stay at the subsistence level and increasingly tend to desert the land in the hope of finding a 'better life' in the cities.

Without culture, agricultural practices cannot be upgraded and industry cannot be established. Culture is primary; it leads by itself to industrial development which, in turn, helps to stimulate culture.

If this is accepted, the strategy of development becomes clear: first and foremost, bring culture into the villages; at the same time, bring industry. (By 'villages' I mean communities with at least a few hundred, but preferably a few thousand inhabitants. Widely scattered hamlets cannot be helped at this stage).

To put this in another way: everything needs a certain 'structure'. Culture needs a consciously evolved structure just as industry needs a consciously evolved structure. In both cases, the 'structure' must be qualitative *and at the same time geographical*, if it is to be a healthy one.

An ideal cultural structure would look like this: a number of cultural 'units' make up the country, each of them containing at least one million and at the most, say, three million inhabitants. Each cultural 'unit' is a pyramid, as follows: primary schools at the village level; a number of villages headed by a market town with a secondary school; a number of market towns headed by a regional centre with an institution of higher learning.

An ideal industrial structure would be essentially similar: small-scale industries in the villages; medium-scale industries in the market towns; large-scale industries in the regional centres; and perhaps a few exceptional and unique industrial activities in the capital city (although this is by no means essential, since the capital city provides in any case certain non-industrial services to the country, which are themselves 'exceptional and unique').

I am not suggesting that such ideal structures are attainable in every case; but they do provide guidelines. It is also obvious that 'industry' is more closely tied to location factors than culture, so that the industrial structure will have to tolerate more 'deviations from the ideal' than the cultural structure.

It must be emphasised that there are no master-key solutions to the problem of healthy development. Gigantic schemes, whether in agriculture, industry, communications, or even in education, may seem attractive in theory but are invariably disastrous in practice. The key to success is not mass production but production by the masses. Any purely economic assessment of a proposed new activity is bound to be misleading, unless the political, sociological, and geographical requirements and prevailing conditions are clearly stated and accepted as terms of reference. The economic calculus by itself always tends to favour the large project as against the small; the urban project as against the rural; the capital-intensive project as against the labour-intensive, because the task of managing machines is always easier than that of managing people. But this simply means that the economic calculus is applicable only *after* the basic policy decisions have been taken. These basic policy decisions should favour the small project as against the large; the rural project as against the urban; the labour-using project as against the capital-using – until labour becomes the effective bottleneck.

Three lines of effort have to be pursued simultaneously in a strategy of healthy development:

(a) bring culture into the rural areas;

(b) bring industrial activities into the rural areas; and

(c) upgrade agricultural methods and practices.

(a) CULTURE

The elements of culture are visual matter, music, reading matter, industrial skills (which will be dealt with separately), and body culture, i.e. hygiene and sport. In all these respects the rural areas are poverty-stricken. To mend this state of affairs demands a great deal of leadership and only a relatively small amount of money.

If Government offices look dilapidated, dirty, and drab, then Government will not be convincing when it calls upon the people to make their houses and villages look smart, clean, and colourful. Self-reliance presupposes a certain pride, and pride grows on the basis of cleanliness and smartness. Whitewashed houses are an asset only if they are kept whitewashed. Wherever possible, bring paint into the villages.

Local art is a major instrument of development. It stimulates the mind, and that is the starting point of everything. Self-made music, which is better than radio, is both a stimulus and an attraction. Most important of all: reading matter. After literacy – what? For every 20 shillings spent on education in literacy, it is worthwhile, and indeed necessary, to spend at least one shilling on the preparation, production, and distribution of reading matter. This must not be confined to utilitarian, instructional material, but must include material of wider scope – political, historical, artistic – a systematic 'Feed-the-Minds Programme'.

Hygiene and sport are equally essential instruments of development. In all these matters, not only the men but also the women need to get involved. If anything, the women are more important than the men, as the next generation is in their care.

How can this be accomplished? It cannot be done by a few education or committee development officers, but only by a systematic involvement of the entire educated population of the developing country.

These few remarks about culture have to be made because it is too often overlooked that culture, and not money, is the primary motive power of development.

The sense of isolation in the rural areas and small towns is intensified by the lack of newspapers and other reading material. The newspapers produced in the capital city normally reach the hinterland only irregularly and often with considerable delay. They are also too expensive. With a bit of local initiative and central support, small local news-sheets could be produced very cheaply.

A successful scheme practised in one developing country was as follows: a number of fairly well educated people from small towns and large villages in the hinterland – mainly school teachers – were given a short training course in the capital. After training, they were supplied with a 'do-it-yourself kit', consisting of a transistor radio (if they did not possess one already), a typewriter, a simple hand-duplicator, and a fair stock of suitable paper. It was arranged that the central radio station would broadcast, three times a week, a News Bulletin at dictation speed. The people trained for this purpose went back to their towns and villages, tuned in at the arranged times, and produced a duplicated news-sheet at minimal expense three times a week. The scheme turned out to be financially self-supporting. In some cases, the local news-sheet producer found it possible to add local news and even editorial matter.

Reading matter is one of the main instruments of culture and, in fact, an indispensable one. Without it, all education is abortive. It can be very cheaply produced. But the contents must be appropriate to the actual conditions of people living in poverty. (People no longer living in poverty have the means to look after themselves). Apart from news, the poor need 'simple messages', that is, small pamphlets with printed matter and visual supports which describe down-to-earth possibilities of self-help and self-improvement – how to build a small feeder road; how to improve one's house; how to feed oneself and the children; how to practice elementary hygiene; also how to paint, make music and so forth.

To produce such 'simple messages' is not easy. Indigenous academics and other intellectuals should organise themselves in small spare-time study groups to prepare them. No one else can do it. But they have to be conscious of the three great gulfs that separate them from the poor in the hinterland and that have to be bridged by compassionate care – the gulf between the rich and the poor; the gulf between the educated and the uneducated; and the gulf between the townsman and the countryman.

(b) Industry

Opportunities for industrial development exist wherever people live together in hundreds or thousands. They also exist wherever valuable raw materials can be found or produced.

Assuming there is an established population of several hundred thousand people, inhabiting a district or region in a not-too-scattered fashion, industrial development depends on the following factors:

(1) Local initiative and will to work along new lines;

(2) Technical know-how, including the knowledge of local natural resources;

(3) Commercial know-how;

(4) Money.

In the rural areas and small towns, all these factors are scarce, and industrial development depends not only on their fullest mobilisation but also on their *systematic, planned supplementation from outside.*

As I have said before, poverty is a vicious circle, and all beginnings are difficult. To look for opportunities for industrial activities means therefore, initially at least, to look for activities in which a beginning has already been made, and to build on them.

The first task is to study what people are already doing – and they must be doing something, otherwise they could not exist – and to help them to do it better, which often means to help them to advance from raw material production into the successive stages of processing.

The second task is to study what people need and to investigate the possibility of helping them to cover more of their needs out of their own productive efforts. It is only when these two tasks have been successfully accomplished that one can safely advance to a third task, that is, to produce new articles destined for markets outside.

Local initiatives for self-help and self-improvement are the most precious asset of all, because without them no organic growth can take place. A population without such initiatives is almost impossible to help. It follows that all such initiatives, wherever they arise, deserve the most careful and sympathetic nurturing and the maximum of outside support.

Appropriate industries in the hinterland will rarely need large amounts of capital, because they will be modest in size and will rarely require more than a few hundred pounds of capital investment per person employed. The lower the average amount of the capital to be found for each industrial workplace, the more workplaces can be created by the investment of a given amount of money. Only by creating a large number of low-cost work places can the problem of mounting unemployment be solved.

It cannot be emphasised too strongly that this is a matter of conscious political choice and not one to be decided by the calculations of economists or businessmen. A country's development policy may be geared primarily to the production of goods or it may be geared primarily to the development of people. The former aims at mass production; the latter, at production by the masses. The former is the inevitable result, if private enterprise is given a free hand, because it is the natural, i.e. rational, desire of the private enterprise employer "to eliminate the human factor", for the simple reason that automated machinery works faster and more reliably than any human being. Feasibility studies undertaken by politically 'neutral' economists will always support this tendency, particularly in a developing country where labour, being unused to industrial work, has yet to be trained. It is then argued that mass production, once successfully established, will benefit the masses by the provision of cheap consumer goods. But since mass production at the level of high capital intensity "eliminates the human factor", the masses find themselves unemployed and unable to buy even the cheapest goods. It is claimed that mass production, if it does find a market, is the most effective instrument for the rapid accumulation of surplus wealth, and that this surplus will then 'percolate' to the unemployed masses. Yet it is a fact of universal experience that no such 'percolation' takes place; a 'dual economy' emerges in which the rich get richer while the poor stagnate or get poorer. Under such auspices, 'self-reliance', 'involvement of the people', and 'development' must remain ineffectual aspirations.

If the political decision is in favour of production by the masses – rather than mass production which "eliminates the human factor" – it follows automatically that the difficult task of developing industrial activities in the hinterland must receive top priority, simply because the mass of the people happen to live in the hinterland and it would be a disaster if they (or even a sizeable proportion of them) were drawn into the capital city. It also follows that industrial developments in the capital city should be strictly confined to two categories, 'national plants' (in certain cases) and small production units serving the local market.

By 'national plants' I mean unique enterprises at a high level of sophistication and capital intensity which for one reason or another cannot be established in the hinterland; an obvious example would be a plant concerned with the servicing of international airliners, but there are no doubt other legitimate cases. Industries in the capital city should be capital-intensive, and labour-saving, because it is not desirable to draw people to the capital city by creating large numbers of industrial workplaces there. Industries in the hinterland should be labour-intensive and capital-saving, because it is desirable to hold the population in the hinterland and give them the chance of acquiring industrial skills.

(c) Agriculture

It is now widely accepted that in the generality of cases farming in a poor country cannot straightaway move from the hoe to the tractor, or from the panga to the combine harvester. An 'intermediate' stage must first be reached and consolidated, utilising equipment that is very much more efficient than hoe or panga and very much cheaper and easier to maintain and utilise than tractor or combine.

The question is: how is the farmer or the farming community to choose the equipment appropriate to their specific needs; how are they to obtain supplies, including spare parts; and how are they to pay for them? The farmer's basic implements are plough, harrow, planter, cultivator, and cart. Some of these can be made by local carpenters, to appropriate specifications, e.g. the harrow and the cart. The others have to be obtained from merchants, who may have to import them. Normally the merchants are unable to offer the farmer a wide enough choice of implements, for instance, of ploughs. Nor is the farmer always in a position to judge which type of plough is suitable for his soil and other circumstances. If he has only two oxen, a plough needing four to six oxen to pull it is a disaster for him. The wrong depth of ploughing may be equally fatal.

In every developing country arrangements along the following lines are required: First, agricultural extension officers need to have at their disposal a whole range of appropriate equipment, such as ploughs, so that, going from farm to farm, they can determine – and demonstrate – which particular type of plough is appropriate to the given conditions. Second, there must be an organisation capable of manufacturing or importing the appropriate equipment, including spare parts, and organising its distribution. There is often no alternative to a governmental organisation undertaking this very urgent task. Third, there is generally a need to increase and intensify the education of farmers in the training of draught animals and the use and maintenance of animal-drawn equipment.

THE HUMAN FACTOR

If healthy development requires a strategy as outlined above – a strategy in which the governments of the developing country have to take all the decisive initiatives – what kind of help can and should be given by the rich countries? It is obvious that it is easy to produce or promote *unhealthy* development – just provide some funds and let things happen as they will. Most of the so-called development will then continue to go into the capital cities; the rich will get richer; the poor, poorer. There will be mass production, instead of production by the masses. The ablest, most progressive, most dynamic and up-to-date business men will "eliminate the human factor" and the economists and statisticians will celebrate splendid 'rates of growth'. All this is relatively easy – and it is the road to a sickness which even the richest societies may find it hard to survive.

But healthy development, with production by the masses instead of mass production, with the cultivation, instead of the elimination, of the human factor, with only modest urbanisation and an organic agro-industrial structure in the hinterland, based on self-reliance and the involvement of the people – that is a different matter. Are we fit to help? Or are we so much caught up in our own system of 'eliminating the human factor' that ours will inevitably and inescapably be the withering touch of which there is so much evidence already?

We can help them with our knowledge, but not with the ways in which we ourselves have utilised and exploited our knowledge. We can help them to solve their problems; if we merely offer them the solutions of *our* problems, we ruin them.

As Professor Myrdal has emphasised in his stupendous work *Asian Drama: An Inquiry into the Poverty of Nations*, the technological advance in the West is very detrimental to the development prospects of the Third World, and there is little hope unless "its unfortunate impact could be counteracted by deliberately increasing research activity and directing it towards problems the solution of which would be in the interest of the under-developed countries".

But who will support those who are struggling to work along such lines? Increasing numbers of people realise that such work is necessary but they do nothing to help it along.

The poor cannot be helped by our giving them methods and equipment which *pre-suppose* a highly developed industrialism. They need an 'intermediate technology'; they need the *stepping stones of self-help*.

Chapter Seven

The Duke
of Buen Consejo

Leopold Kohr

How to turn a teeming slum into a splendid little city through 'nuclear seeding'.

Many of the potential beauty spots in Greater San Juan are slums, with the result that what our socially but not aesthetically conscious planners usually see in them is slums, not beauty. And all they can think of when they see slums is to lather them with disinfectant soap and shave them away. Instead of bringing out their quality as almost ideal centres of urban life, they tend to claim absolution from their sins when they replace them with either traffic circles or parks. This is what is planned with La Perla, with El Fanguito, with the region near Esquife, with Buen Consejo, with everything.

Slums are of course medically unhealthy, and they do constitute an economic problem. But socially and urbanely they have solved problems which their earnest redevelopers have attacked in vain in the modern urbanisations taking place. In their warm heaving humanity there is no solitude for the old, no lack of supervision for the young; and what often surprises visitors if they come without their textbooks is not their poverty, which is great, but the happiness which seems to radiate from it all. In many ways they seem to be the answer to the man who was told he could find happiness if a happy man would let him have his shirt. But no one he approached, from prince to archbishop, to millionaire and, undoubtedly the psychoanalyst, to social worker, claimed to be happy until in his despair he turned to a beggar. He was the first to admit he was happy – and he owned no shirt.

However, the high degree of social happiness aside, what slum dwellers demonstrate from an urban point of view is, above all, that they are one of five blessed categories of people endowed with what seems to have completely withered away in modern site selectors and city planners under the impact of their traffic obsessed indoctrination. They have a marvellous sense of location. The other four categories are the aristocrats, the inn-keepers, the military, and the Church. They all choose their sites with the instinct with which birds choose their nests, without the benefit of consultants from famous technological institutes. As a result, where they pitch their tents, there it is good to live. And where it is good to live, it is also beautiful to live.

Instead of erasing the slums, our planners should therefore mine their beauty, redeem them, and build them up. That is what the Venetians did, or the inhabitants of Assisi. They all started as slum dwellers. But as they prospered, they did not, as we would nowadays do in our neurotic status-seeking habits, desert the hovels that were miserable but still were their homes. They began to beautify them. They turned mud into wood, and wood into slums. And those who became more affluent would fuse their huts with those of their neighbours, turn stone into marble, and houses into palaces, until stale lagoon waters such as El Fanguito's became the Canale Grande of Venice, and a slum hill such as Buen Consejo the gleaming hilltop town of Assisi, its patrician squares and splendid churches a befitting monument to the unfailing taste and sense of location of both the Church of the Renaissance and the Saint of the Poor.

There is another reason why slums should be redeemed rather than cleared, and why the designs used as teaching models for urban reconstruction should be patterned on the exquisite lacework of La Perla rather than the multicoloured artificialities from the drawing boards of engineering colleges. This is that, with their instinctive sense for the aesthetic element of urban location, slum dwellers are not only superb in spotting the choicest sites. They are also unsurpassed in the way they arrange in the most functional fashion their trades and occupations, their communal and residential structures. Grouping them like the notes of a gaily whistled melody around widening squares and narrowing footpaths, and utilising every inch to good purpose, they capture their residents in a breathtaking variety of dramatic settings: on stilts in glistening waters, up along the ridges of steep cliffs, or down the natural flows of twisting gullies and eddies chattering and gurgling like mountain streams. This is the medley of pedestrian on-the-spot living which our unfortunate planners are forever trying to eliminate. Yet, it is precisely this that breeds in all its economic and hygienic shortcomings the substance of communal happiness.

But being communities of a single social layer, slums are of course as lopsided, incomplete, and ineffective in their capacity as traffic absorbers and velocity-reducing catalysts as are the suburbs of millionaires; and what they need if their intrinsic beauty of location is to be used for contracting them into inner directed rival cities is the same that is need in the case of old San Juan. Their aesthetically rich soil must be seeded with a small nucleus of persons of discriminating taste and sufficient social attractive power to draw after them the remaining layers of the amenities of the good life...

I have often meant to write what the Germans call a *Staatsroman* – a state novel, an exercise in literary fiction for the purpose of illuminating the implications of a social theory. The most likely location for my prospected *Staatsroman* is the teeming slum hill of Buen Consejo at the edge of the metropolitan area of San Juan. Having been selected not by experts from MIT but by slum dwellers, the site is, not surprisingly, so stunning that it would satisfy even the most demanding sense of residential and commercial location. It certainly has greatly enlivened the planning languor of my dreams. Moreover, it has a singularly charming name – *Buen Consejo*, Good Advice. I have not yet decided on the sort of Machiavellian love interest that should be instilled into the story. But I have a rather clear idea as to the rest of the plot. And above all, I have the title: *The Duke of Buen Consejo.*

Even as it is, Buen Consejo has all the makings of a splendid little city, and I often point them out to visitors who are at first bewildered, then amused, and finally enraptured, once they succeed in seeing the exquisite beauty underneath a seemingly unappetising surface. Cascading down the slopes of a steep hill, its buzzing streets run joyfully into the eddies of dozens of leisurely squares hanging like flower-bedecked balconies over gullies, houses, and valleys. Its footpaths, created by the movement of life itself, wind naturally up and down, often abruptly ending in daring flights of stairs leading skywards to dramatically posed houses musing like exotic birds on slender legs high above the reach of cars and controversy. Its views sweep out over the neighbouring communities below, over the tree-lined mirror-still eyes of enigmatic lagoons in the distance, and on the foaming white horses of the surf until they become indistinct in the shimmering blue expanse of the ocean on the horizon. The whole settlement looks rather like the cone of Mont Saint Michel, San Marino, Fiesole or, on a smaller scale, like Segovia or Toledo – except, of course that it is an abysmal slum. But so were once also the others. And like the others in their still crowded quarters. It is full of the radiant hum of warm-hearted people, sun-bathed and wind-cooled, happy in the cooperative closeness of their communal existence, and safe in the sovereignty of their huts, the drowsy refuge of their individuality.

Now, instead of shaving Buen Consejo off the surface of the earth and turning it into another wooded park into which no one will ever set foot again; or instead of waiting for decades until a welfare-minded anxious government, which after all has the whole of Puerto Rico as its concern, will at last come around to allocating the necessary funds within the slowtrickling priority scale of a sweepingly comprehensive national plan; my *Staatsroman* envisions the Governor entrusting the improvement of this particular community – along with the local rather than national development of a host of similar communities – to a private entrepreneur. Since the reason for this is the inescapable insufficiency of public funds necessary for the simultaneous pursuit of a great number of development programs of equal urgency (as otherwise the government would of course undertake the task itself), it follows that the private entrepreneur to be put in charge of Buen Consejo must be able to finance the expected improvements out of his own pocket. In other words, he must be a person of means, a capitalist of substance, a millionaire many times over.

However, in spite of the pathetic ambition to excel in social service rather than private gain, which our mass age has imposed on the intimidated tribe of modern welfare-capitalists, it is doubtful whether a rich man such as a Rockefeller or a Luis Ferré could be enticed into assuming a task of this scope. For whatever it might contribute to his reputation as a benefactor of mankind, he knows that he would still be abused, and have his motives doubted, by the Marxists, by the cynics, by the politicians, by the academics, by the psychologists, by the beneficiaries, by the editors, by the competitors, by Krushchev quoting the gospel and, from far beyond the grave, by the voice of Adam Smith quoting from *The Wealth of Nations*. He would therefore have to be offered a more concrete inducement than mere honour or pretended acclaim, an inducement derived not from his sense of social responsibility but from the always reliable old-fashioned human motivation of pride, vanity, self-interest.

Money, however, would in this case not work for a variety of reasons. The public has none to offer, the millionaire has enough and, if he *should* be accessible to the lure of additional riches, he would obviously choose more profitable targets for investment than the building of modern accommodations for impoverished slum dwellers. But there are other incentives compellingly stirring the private interest. What a millionaire entrepreneur might not wish to undertake for the sake of an extra million, he might, as England has so fruitfully demonstrated, assume for the sake of a vanity-flattering high sounding aristocratic title. There are many rich people in the world, but very few of them who are dukes. So, in order to arouse the necessary enthusiasm, the governor of my story decides not only to commission a rich millionaire with executing the novel's featured local development project; he confers this project on him as a duchy. He makes him the duke of Buen Consejo.

That Puerto Rico is a Republic should not stand in the way of such titles any more than it does in San Marino which is a republic too – the oldest, in fact, in the world, going all the way back to the year 300 A.D. Yet, republic or not, San Marino has enriched both its incorruptible treasury and its looks to a not inconsiderable degree by conferring elegant aristocratic titles on wealthy foreigners. However, to produce really the desired result, the dukedom of Buen Consejo would have to convey more than a mere title worn by an absentee patron saint. Like the dukedoms of history, it would have to be invested with a high degree of sovereignty, or with suzerainty under the authority of the national government. Its Duke would therefore actually be the executive head of the new domain, not quite like the Prince of Monaco, but almost. This would have the additional advantage of attracting so many applicants that the Governor would have no difficulty finding candidates possessing not only appropriate riches but also appropriate ability.

Taking this as starting point, the rest of the story is self-developing. Being a duke, he must have an appropriately splendid residence. And being the head of a community, this residence must be located not at the outskirts of Buen Consejo but in its very midsts. Like the White House, Fortaleza, or Buckingham Palace, it will serve as both government centre and private home. The Duke will therefore hardly need to be prodded into embellishing it. Moreover, unlike a stern republican government, he will be able to abandon himself to the ego-swelling and beauty-generating principle of conspicuous consumption, which has contributed so much to the sensuous splendour of the renaissance cities rather than having to pay homage to the puritanical sterility of the nowadays so fashionable principle of conspicuous abstention, which may enhance the moral stature of its practitioners, but hardly the aesthetic value of their communities. Buen Consejo will make such creative indulgence all the more possible as, contrary to modern theory, the social acceptability of conspicuous consumption varies inversely with the wealth of the public. The poorer a society, the more will its members delight in being represented by pomp and circumstance. The richer – the more will they demand of their leaders the public display of impecunious humility as a guilt-ridden sign of their collective penance for a private affluence they are morally incapable of accepting as deserved.

Thus, Buen Consejo's first ducal development project serves not the slummers but the Duke. No public funds have been used, no money but his own. However, one can imagine the pains of his delicate Duchess, now that she has come to live on the spot. As she looks out from her damask curtained room of gilded mirrors and embroidered tapestries, all she sees is a muddy square surrounded by huts made of cardboard and compressed sardine tins. Lest he lose his lovely wife, the Duke realises he must do more than just provide her with a palace. He must adorn the approaches.

His second development project will therefore be paving the square. With this, his private gain begins for the first time to produce an asset automatically benefiting also the community. However since, from his point of view, the paving is nonetheless primarily still meant to serve a mere decorative extension of his private palace, its cost is still chargeable to his personal account. Moreover, precisely because he has his own rather than the as yet insensitive public interest in mind, he will, like the Medicis before him, execute the paving project not in utilitarian republican concrete but in aristocratic marble. This, in turn, will set the tone also for the other squares, though in their case the improvement will no longer be financed from the Duke's private funds. However, this will not impede their rapid embellishment. For, as history has so often shown, many of the things that are beyond the financial reach of prosperous, integrated, costly superpowers, constitute no budgetary problems in poor communities as long as they are small. The famous savings of scale are all on their side, of small scale that is, with no public need to provide their citizens with, and make them financially responsible for, an average stretch of 13.4 miles of four-lane super dual carriage way per each and every man.

But even a square paved with marble will not be enough to satisfy the aesthetic sophistication of the Duchess. So His Serene Highness will, as his next step, induce his tin-shacked neighbours to rebuild their homes, with the help of appropriate subsidies, in a material and style benefiting the new environment. In fact, aroused by his example, many of them will already have begun to do precisely this on their own initiative, so that the required subsidies will be so insignificant as to leave hardly a dent in the ducal treasury. The principal need will be for aesthetic and technical rather than financial assistance. Moreover, considering that the new wave of beautification benefits from now on quite tangibly no longer only the Duke but everyone whose property borders on the recently marbled square, the neighbours will also on this ground be quite willing to bear the bulk of the improvement costs themselves. The only question is: can they? After all, as slum dwellers they are still abjectly poor. But they are poor because for centuries they have held in their hands the costliest of all development resources, labour power, without ever putting it to proper use. Bearing the bulk of the costs themselves means therefore no more than at last using properly the one commodity over which they dispose in abundance already.

As a result, the second phase of urban renewal, though it involves by now also a large degree of public improvement, is again executed by means of strictly private resources, mobilised in addition no longer by the Duke alone but jointly with his aroused and equally benefiting neighbours. In other words, the second phase represents from an economic point of view actually less of a problem than the first. All that is at this juncture required of the Duke is to inject a relatively small amount of his personal embellishment funds into the plaza outside his residence. As this is the focal point at which his own private interests intersect with those of his neighbours, and the interests of both with those of the public, an infusion at this strategic location will suffice to trigger off such chain reaction of supplementary private activities that the marbled square will soon be transformed into an effective urban nucleus – without the need for tapping a penny in public funds. And the process will of course not stop here. For once the stimulus of outside help, however small at its origin, has released the tremendous dormant forces of self-help, it will spread from square to square, and street to street until nothing is left of the slum except its exquisite geography. Moreover, fanned by the spirit of both emulation and competition, the whole dramatic development will not be the wearisome product of cautiously phased successive stages of a long-run plan ceremoniously unfolding in majestic lethargy, but of a number of brief simultaneous bursts of energy erupting with volcanic ferocity in all corners of the place at the same time.

The third development phase now setting in has a more sophisticated objective. Evolving naturally out of the second, it is primarily concerned with the task of introducing variety into that deadly pattern of uniformity which is not only the inevitable result of all central planning, but the most characteristic feature of all slums, the slums of affluence no less than those of poverty. But once again, the program that might be beyond the reach of super powers will prove practically self-generating as well as self-financing in the Duchy of Buen Consejo. In fact, ducal funds may now no longer be needed at all. For the burst of activities which has enlivened the second phase has raised the Duchy's income level-sufficiently to supply it with the development funds for the third. And the same activities that have produced the required funds have also prepared the ground for variety to sprout forth. For the basically uncoordinated self-help and laissez-faire character of the majority of these activities have resulted in the gradual assertion of a multitude of differences in taste, temperament, and skill not only architecturally, but also socially, professionally, and economically.

Following the aesthetic lead of the Duke, or rather perhaps the Duchess, but otherwise exclusively engaged in the pursuit of their own varied interests, some citizens have thus begun to build taller, some smaller. Some are staying workers, some are becoming craftsmen. Some are rising in affluence, some are lagging behind. With the increase in personal involvements, some decide to become psychoanalysts, some priests. Moreover, following the Duke's example, the rising middle class, instead of escaping once again into the costly unurban boredom of the suburbs, considers it smart to live on its business premises. This infuses into the picture an additional dimension in architectural differences, making a number of houses so stately that some of them are beginning to rival even the residence of the Duke. The same process will affect ecclesiastical buildings, with the Church zestfully assuming its traditional role as pace setter in glorious architecture and as discriminating patron of the arts. This, in turn, creates opportunities for anarchistic diversity of artists. And artists must of course sit in cafés which, adjusting to the new social scene, and bursting out into varying styles and degrees of luxury, are adding the last in convivial amenities by spilling gaily over the sidewalks along leisurely streets whose vehicular traffic has become largely dispensable under the dense pedestrian living conditions surviving as one of the principal social luxuries from the original slum.

All this is quite contrary to modern planning ideals which are trying their best not to emphasise but to level differences. But luckily our Duke does not subscribe to them. He thinks that the good city is not the uniform but the diverse city; not a diffuse flatland at whatever high a plateau, but a pyramid rising from a sharply defined base in exciting progression through a series of narrowing tiers up towards the sky. He knows with Aristotle that "a state is not made up only of so many men, but of different kinds of men; for similars do not constitute a state. It is not like a military alliance". And he agrees with Gilbert and Sullivan when they say of a fiesta to which only *grandees* are admitted: "where everybody is somebody, nobody is anybody".

With the aesthetic, economic, and material conditions improved, we have arrived at the final phase of development. This concerns itself with more than mere urban renewal. It aims at the culminating target: the raising of the Duchy's educational level. This is again in contradiction to conventional development patterns, most of which attempt to educate first and improve material conditions later. But our Duke has long realised that premature education is as much of an obstacle to rapid development as no education. For the educated man has higher wage claims and other requirements than an underproductive underdeveloped community can afford. Provoking claims on a national product that does as yet not exist, premature education must therefore necessarily lead to frustration rather than satisfaction; to a painful disequilibrium rather than a new equilibrium at a higher level; to an increase in costs when the belt-tightening nature of all progress demands that costs should be kept low; to strikes when all hands should be put to work.

But now the time is ripe for achieving the cultural crowning mission of the ducal reign. As we have seen, one of the few constitutional restrictions imposed on the group stipulates that he and his family must maintain their regular residence within the boundaries of the Duchy. This makes it impossible for His Serene Highness to send his children away from Buen Consejo when they reach school age. Since he is nevertheless anxious to provide them with the best possible education, he has no alternative but to bring the best teachers in at his own expense. And since he is also anxious to raise his children in the most normal fashion, he will not content himself with importing the best teachers. He will also set them up in appropriately endowed and appointed schools to which also the children of the poorest will be admitted free of charge. This will bring a measure of democratic roughage to the wealthy and the sophistication of aristocracy to the poor, until all social layers of Buen Consejo will have become culturally so demanding and economically so strong that they will not only begin to produce the best teachers themselves; they will also be able to bring forth and support the last and most elevated tier of cultural producers, the philosophers, the poets, the composers, as well as the small concert house and the intimate theatre in which they can perform.

And, once again, even at this culminating level, the cost of it all will constitute a negligible problem. Given an initial push from the private purse of the Duke, furnished for reasons of strictly personal improvement, it will in its subsequent and more demanding stages easily be borne by the community itself, not because it will then be producing so much but because – as in the case of every small enterprise – the cost of running it will be so little. In other words, Buen Consejo will be able to finance its culture simply by not having to finance (a) the kind of bureaucracy-infested government machinery that is necessary to keep a large society integrated with its own extremities; and (b) the prohibitively expensive road network necessary to prevent it from losing track of itself, to say nothing of all the impoverishing and privately borne incidentals such a roadwork entails: the cars racing endlessly up and down in a vain effort to pull abreast of forever increasing technological distances; the repair work keeping the cars in shape; and the petrol quenching their unquenchable thirst.

Utopian? Hardly! A utopia promises the abolition of all misery. What Buen Consejo offers is the utterly realistic advantages of small size. Being so much smaller than most modern political communities, it will quite naturally *minimise* the problems of life in common. And it will minimise them at a geometric rate so that they will be more in line with the small stature of man. But it will *solve* none of them, that is none except the main problem of our age, the problem of excessive size. In wholly un-utopian fashion, it accepts the imperfections in both man and society as they are.

It will therefore still have its quantum of disease, passion, frustration, intrigue, violence, idiocy, trickery. And, for all I know, my story may end with a satiated citizenry reverting to the solid old forms of a no-nonsense republican government by ungratefully dismissing the Duke once he has fulfilled his vital development function, perhaps even beheading him, and in a dignified ceremony, commemorating his fruitful reign by naming a zestful pub or a night club *The Duke's Head* (following in this the lead of the restrained English who, while taking their pleasures sadly, as Voltaire once remarked, seem not infrequently intent upon taking their executions gladly).

But I have still an unpuritanical open mind about this. I may keep the Duke. After all, one of the strongest forces of cohesion, particularly during the harassing times of economic development and social change, is precisely a personal, ducal, monarchical centre, a paternalistic father image, that radiates trust along with the indispensable authority, and rules by setting an example rather than by imposing conduct through decree. It makes many things so much simpler and cheaper. As we have seen, all our Duke must do if there is need for stimulating a subsequently self-generating desire for general education is to make his people the witness of his educational concern for his own family. To instil into them a sense for elegance and style, the pace setting habits of the Duchess will be as effective as costly appreciation courses. To arouse their enthusiasm for the theatre and the arts, he must but display a conspicuous interest in them himself, as did the Duke of Weimar in Goethe's time, as a result of which the lowliest coachman and humblest maid became as familiar with the latest achievements in literature as they would now be with the twist. And to push economic development, all he must do is engage in a display of conspicuous consumption which, far from being socially reprehensible, performs the same function as a national fair, a fashion show, or a Sears & Roebuck catalogue. It informs the people from the most strategic centre of what is going on, and advertises what is being produced. Indeed, so valuable are monarchical symbols as tools of efficient salesmanship, that an editor from the *Economist* came justly to the conclusion after perusing American advertisements that the United States is the country most devoted to the crown.

So I may keep the Duke right to the happy end, rather than restore Buen Consejo to the folds of the republic whose codes are most honourable. But they do tend to hound every representative public person seen stepping from his official car into a night club until he abdicates or descends into the shadows of conspicuous abstention. Which may qualify him for holy orders. But in times of development, it is economically about as beneficial as a frugal government bent on the sterility of saving rather than on spending.

Fiction? I have called it a *Staatsroman*. It is a *Roman* as far as Buen Consejo is concerned, with its heroes and heroics unfortunately indeed bearing hardly any resemblance to living persons or incidents. But otherwise it is nothing of the kind. It pictures not theory but history as it unfolded itself in a vast number of villages, cities, and city states all over Europe during the Middle Ages, or in the countless urban foundations of Greek and Phoenician antiquity. They all were developed through nuclear seeding rather than comprehensive planning. And they, too, were for ages milling around at stagnant substandard levels, hoping for something to come to their assistance, until they became possessed by a tyrant, a lord, an aristocratic merchant, a duke, a prince, a king, who decided that what was needed was not a subtle economic growth machinery but a bit of aesthetic ambition; that the fast way of advancing is not by waiting for outside help but by doing things oneself; that the point is not that communities cannot build because they are poor, but that they are poor because the bastards won't build; not that they must have union before they can afford luxuries, but that they must have reached a level of luxury before they can afford the expensive parasitism of union.

So simple is the economics of development on a local rather than a national and international scale, and so great the scale advantage of small size, that a whole battery of nuclear seeders has historically often appeared in a number of hotly competing city states at the same time, and done severally what no great power could ever have achieved unitedly in such a chain reaction of duplicating efforts: raising their domains from slum to marble often in the brief creative spasm of a single generation. When Peisistratos appeared on the scene, the major part of Athens consisted of hovels. When he departed, there stood the array of buildings of whose immortal beauty Pausanias could write hundreds of years later that, when they were new, they already looked ancient. Now that they were old, they still looked new. Similarly, Venice started her scintillating career as an abysmal slum. Had she followed modern advice and waited with her development until Italy had been united, the United Nations established, the Common Market formed, she would still be a slum today. And so would Urbino, Perugia, Assisi, Parma, Padua, and most of the glamorous rest. By going ahead on her own in the fashion of the Duke of Buen Consejo, she violated all principles of sound politics, economics, planning, location theory, indeed of intellectual levelheadedness itself. For who except a fool or bohemian slummer would build in the midst of a lagoon. But she gave us Venice.

Chapter Eight

The New Economics

E. F. Schumacher

I was brought up on an interpretation of history which suggested that everything started with a few families and the families got together in tribes; a bit later a lot of tribes joined together into nation states; the nation states became bigger and bigger and formed great regional combinations, 'United States of this', 'United States of that', and finally we could look forward to a single World Government.

Ever since I heard this plausible story I have been observing what is actually happening, and I have seen a proliferation of countries. The United Nations started twenty years ago with about 50 or 60 members, now there are 120 and the number is still growing. In my youth, this was called 'Balkanisation' and was thought to be a very bad thing. But what I have been witnessing, over the last 50 years in any case, is a very high degree of Balkanisation all over the place, that is to say, large units breaking up into smaller units. Well, it makes you think. Not that everything that happens is necessarily right; but I am sure we should at least notice that it is happening.

Secondly I was brought up on a theory which claimed that in order to be prosperous a country had to be very big, the bigger the better. Look at what Churchill called "the pumper-nickel principalities of Germany", and then look at the Bismarkian Reich: is it not obvious that the great prosperity of Germany only became possible through this combination? All the same, if we make a list of all the most prosperous countries in the world, we find that in overwhelming majority they are very very small; and if you make a list of the largest countries of the world, most of them are exceedingly poor. This again gives one some food for thought.

And thirdly I was brought up on the theory of the economics of scale, that, just as with nations so with business and industries, there is an irresistible trend, dictated by modern technology, for the scale of business organisation to become ever bigger. Now, it is quite true that today there are business organisations that are probably bigger than anything known before in history; but the number of small units is not declining even in countries like the United States and many of these small units are extremely prosperous, and provide society with most of the really fruitful new developments. So the situation is no doubt a puzzling one for anyone who has been brought up the way I and most of my age group have been.

We are told, even today, that gigantic organisations are inescapably necessary, but where they have in fact been created, what happens? Take General Motors: The great achievement of Mr Sloan of General Motors was to structure this gigantic firm in such a manner that it became in fact, a federation of firms, none of them gigantic. And in my own shop, the National Coal Board, which is the biggest 'firm' in Europe, we are doing something very similar. Strenuous efforts are being made to structure it in such a way that, while remaining one big organisation, it operates and feels like a federation of what we call 'quasifirms'. Instead of a monolith, it becomes a well co-ordinated assembly of lively, semi-autonomous units, each with its own drive and sense of achievement. While many pure theoreticians (who one suspects may not be very closely in touch with reality) are engaging in the idolatry of large size, in the actual world there is a tremendous push and surge to profit from the convenience, humanity and manageability of small size. So much about what anyone can easily observe for himself.

Let us now approach our subject from another angle and ask what is *needed*. As in so many other respects, if one looks a bit more deeply one always finds that at least two things are needed for human life which appear, on the face of it, to be contradictory. We need freedom and order: the freedom of lots and lots of small units and the orderliness of large-scale, possibly global, organisation. When it comes to action, we obviously need small-scale organisation, because action is a highly personal affair, and one cannot be in touch with more than a limited number of persons at any one time. But when it comes to ideology or to ethics, to the world of ideas, we have to operate in terms of a world-wide unity. Or to put it differently, it is true that all men are brothers, but it is also true that when we want to act, in our active personal relations, we can in fact be in touch only with very few of them. And we all know people who freely talk about the brotherhood of man while treating all their neighbours as enemies – just as we know people who have, in fact, excellent relations with their neighbours, but are at the same time full of the most appalling prejudices about all human groups outside their own particular circle. What I mean to emphasise is our dual requirement: there cannot be a unified solution of all human problems. For his different purposes man needs many different organisations, both small and large ones, both exclusive and comprehensive. Yet people find it most difficult to keep two apparently opposite necessities of truth in their minds at the same time. They always look for a final solution; they insist that it must be a matter of either-or, either you must be in favour of small-scale or in favour of large-scale. It is therefore normally the task of the people who want to do constructive work, not to plug one particular thing, but to restore some kind of balance. The restoration of balance that I believe is needed in our situation today implies a fight against the prevailing idolatry of giantism. (If there were an idolatry in the opposite direction, namely that *all* large organisations were the work of the devil, then one would have to push in the opposite direction).

The question of scale might be put in another way: what is needed in all these matters is to discriminate, to get things sorted out. For every activity there is a certain appropriate scale, and the more active and intimate the activity, the smaller the number of people that can take part, the greater is the number of such relationship arrangements that need to be established. Take teaching: one listens to all sorts of extraordinary debates about the superiority of the University of the Air, or the teaching machine over some other forms of teaching. Well, let us discriminate: what are we trying to teach? It then becomes immediately apparent that certain things can only be taught in a very intimate circle, whereas other things can obviously be taught en mass, via the air, via television, via teaching machines, and so on.

What scale is appropriate? It depends on what we are trying to do. The question of scale is extremely crucial today, in political, social and economic affairs just as in almost everything else. What, for instance, is the appropriate size of a city? And also, one might ask, what is the appropriate size of a country? Now these are serious and difficult questions. It is not possible to programme a computer and get the answer. The really serious matters of life cannot be calculated. We cannot directly calculate what is right; but we jolly well know what is wrong! We can recognise right and wrong at the extremes, although we cannot normally judge them finely enough to say: "This ought to be five per cent more; or that ought to be five per cent less".

Take the question of size of a city. While one cannot judge these things with precision, I think it is fairly safe to say that the upper limit of what is desirable for the size of a city is probably something of the order of half a million. It is quite clear that above such a size nothing is added to the virtue of the city. In places like London, or Tokyo, or New York, the millions do not add to the city's real value but merely create *enormous* problems and produce human degradation. So probably the order of magnitude of five hundred thousand inhabitants could be looked upon as the upper limit. The question of the lower limit of a real city, is much more difficult to judge. The finest cities in history have been very small by 20th Century standards. The instruments and institutions of city culture depend, no doubt, on a certain accumulation of wealth. But how much wealth has to be accumulated depends on the type of culture pursued. Philosophy, the arts and religion cost very very little money. Other types of what claims to be 'high culture', space research or ultra-modern physics cost a lot of money, but are somewhat remote from the real needs of men.

I raise the question of the proper size of cities because, to my mind, this is the most relevant point when we come to consider the most desirable size of nations. I know one cannot draw the map as one sees fit, but it is still legitimate to ask what is the right size of a nation: and this question is closely inter-related with the question of the proper size of cities. Why? This idolatry of giantism that I have talked about is, of course, based on modern technology, particularly as it concerns transport and communications. It has one immensely powerful effect: it makes people *footloose*. Millions of people start moving about, deserting the rural areas and the smaller towns to follow the city lights, to go to the big city, causing a pathological growth. Take the country in which all this is perhaps most exemplified, the United States. Sociologists are studying the problem of 'megalopolis'. The word 'metropolis' is no longer big enough; hence, 'megalopolis'. They freely talk about the polarisation of the population of the United States into three immense mega-lopolitan areas: one extending from Boston to Washington, a continuous built-up area, with sixty million people; one around Chicago, another sixty million; and one on the West Coast, from San Francisco to San Diego, again a continuous built-up area with sixty million people; the rest of the country being left practically empty; deserted provincial towns, and the land cultivated with vast tractors, combine harvesters, and immense amounts of chemicals.

If this is somebody's conception of the future of the United States, it is hardly a future worth having. But whether we like it or not, this is the result of people having become footloose; it is the result of that marvellous mobility of labour which economists treasure above all else. Let me try an analogy: a large cargo ship can travel the stormy seas with comparative safety, *provided its load is secured*; if the load becomes mobile, becomes 'footloose', then the ship will surely founder. Or let's look at it this way: everything in this world has to have a *structure*, otherwise it is chaos. Before we had mass transport and mass communications, the structure was simply there, because people were relatively immobile. People who absolutely wanted to move were in fact amazingly mobile, witness the great floods of saints from Ireland moving all over Europe. There were communications; there was mobility; but there was no footlooseness. The impact of modern technology upon the existing structure has made it collapse. There is no more structure. A country is like a big cargo ship in which the load is in no way secured: it tilts one way, and all the load slips that way, and the ship founders.

One of the chief elements of structure for the whole of mankind is of course *the state*. And one of the chief elements or instruments of structuralisation (if I may use that term), are *frontiers*, national frontiers. Now previously, before this technological intervention, the relevance of frontiers was almost exclusively political and dynastic; frontiers were delimitations of political power, determining how many people you could raise for war. Economists fought against such frontiers becoming economic barriers – hence the ideology of free trade. But, then, people and things were not footloose; transport was expensive enough so that movements, both of people and of goods, were never more than marginal. Trade in the pre-industrial era was not a trade in essentials, but a trade in precious stones, precious metals, luxury goods, spices. The basic requirements of life had of course to be indigenously produced. And the movement of populations, except in periods of disaster, was confined to persons who had a very special reason to move, such as the Irish saints or the scholars of the University of Paris.

But now everything and everybody has become mobile. All structures are threatened, and all structures are *vulnerable* to an extent that they have never been before. Doctors and psychologists speak of modern society as 'the stress society'. When life is so much easier and the standard of life so much higher than ever before, why should there be a 'stress society'? Because anything that happens, anywhere in the wide wide world, can blow you off course. A business may be sound today; people have learnt it; people have settled down to it – something happens somewhere in the world, and tomorrow it is uneconomic and has to be wiped out. All this, I suggest, is the result of the 'footlooseness' produced by swift and cheap transport and instantaneous communications.

Economics, which Lord Keynes had hoped would settle down as a modest occupation, similar to dentistry, suddenly becomes the most important subject of all. Economic policies absorb almost the entire attention of government, and at the same time government becomes ever more impotent. The simplest things, which only fifty years ago one could see to without difficulty cannot get done any more. The richer a society, the more impossible it becomes to do worthwhile things without immediate pay-off. Economics has become such a thraldom that it absorbs almost the whole of foreign policy. People say 'ah yes, we don't like to go with these people, but we depend on them economically so we must humour them'. It tends to absorb the whole of ethics and to take precedence over all other human considerations. Now, quite clearly, this is a pathological development, which has, of course, many roots, but one of its clearly visible roots lies in the great achievements of modern technology in terms of transport and communications.

While people, with an easy-going kind of logic, believe that fast transport and instantaneous communications open up a new dimension of freedom, (which they do in some rather trivial respects), they overlook the fact that these achievements also tend to destroy freedom, by making everything extremely vulnerable and extremely insecure, unless – please note – unless conscious policies are developed and conscious action is taken, to mitigate the destructive effects of these technological developments.

Now, these destructive effects are obviously most severe in *large* countries, because, as we have seen, frontiers produce 'structure', and it is a much bigger decision for someone to cross a frontier, to uproot himself from his native land and try and put down roots in another land, than to move within the frontiers of his country. The factor of footlooseness is, therefore, the more serious, the bigger the country. Its destructive effects can be traced both in the rich and in the poor countries. In the rich countries such as the United States of America, it produces, as already mentioned, 'megalopolis'. It also produces a rapidly increasing and ever more intractable problem of 'drop-outs', of people who, having become footloose, cannot find a place anywhere in society. Directly connected with this, it produces an appalling problem of crime, alienation, stress, social breakdown, right down to the level of the family. In the poor countries, again most severely in the largest ones, it produces mass migration into cities, mass unemployment, and, as the vitality is drained out of the rural areas, the threat of famine. The result is a 'dual society' without any inner cohesion, subject to a maximum of political instability.

As an illustration, let me take the case of Peru. The capital city of Peru, Lima, situated on the Pacific coast, had a population of 175,000 in the early twenties, just over forty years ago. Its population is now approaching three million. The once beautiful Spanish city is now infested with slums, surrounded by misery-belts that are crawling up the Andes. But this is not all. People are arriving from the rural areas at the rate of a thousand a day – and nobody knows what to do with them. The social, or psychological structure of life in the hinterland has collapsed; people have become footloose and arrive in the capital city at the rate of a thousand a day to squat on some empty land, against the police who come to beat them out, to build their mud hovels and look for a job. *And nobody knows what to do about them.* Nobody knows how to stop the drift.

So, when everybody and everything becomes footloose, the *idea of structure* becomes a really central idea, to which all our powers of thought and imagination must be applied, and, as I said, a primary instrument of structure is the nation state with its frontiers. A large country, I am quite certain, can survive this age of footlooseness only if it achieves a highly articulated *internal* structure, so that in fact it becomes a loose federation of relatively small states, each with its own capital city capable of offering all the culture and facilities which only a city can offer, *including government.* A city without government is obviously second-rate. But how can small countries be 'viable'?

Imagine that in 1864 Bismark had annexed the whole of Denmark instead of only a small part of it, and that nothing had happened since. The Danes would be an ethnic minority in Germany, perhaps struggling to maintain their language by becoming bilingual, the official language of course being German. Only by thoroughly Germanising themselves could they avoid being second-class citizens. There would be an irresistible drift of the most ambitious and enterprising Danes, thoroughly Germanised, to the mainland in the South, and what then would be the status of Copenhagen? That of a remote provincial city. Or imagine Belgium a part of France suddenly turned what is now charmingly called 'nats' wanting independence. There would be endless, heated arguments that these 'non-countries' could not be economically viable, that their desire for independence was, to quote a famous political commentator, "adolescent emotionalism, political naivety, phoney economics, and sheer bare-faced opportunism".

How can one talk about the economics of small independent countries? How can one discuss a problem that is a non-problem? There is no such thing as the viability of states or of nations, there is only a problem of viability of people: people, actual persons like you and me, they are viable when they can stand on their own feet and earn their keep. You do not make non-viable people viable by putting large numbers of them into one huge community, and you do not make viable people non-viable by splitting a large community into a number of smaller, more intimate, more coherent and more manageable groups. All this is perfectly obvious and there is absolutely nothing to argue about. Some people ask: "What happens when a country, composed of one rich province and several poor ones falls apart because the rich province secedes?" Most probably the answer is: "Nothing very much happens". The rich will continue to be rich and the poor will continue to be poor. "But if, before secession, the rich province has subsidised the poor, what happens then?" Well then, of course, the subsidy might stop. But the rich rarely subsidise the poor; more often they exploit them. They may not do so directly so much as through the terms of trade. They may obscure the situation a little by a certain redistribution of tax revenue or small scale charity, but the last thing they want to do is secede from the poor.

The normal case is quite different, namely that the poor provinces wish to separate from the rich, and that the rich want to hold on because they know that exploitation of the poor within one's own frontiers is infinitely easier than exploitation of the poor beyond them. Now if a poor province wishes to secede at the risk of losing some mythical subsidies, what attitude should one take?

Not that we have to decide this, but what should we think about it? Is it not a wish to be applauded and respected? Do we want people to stand on their own feet, as free and self-reliant men? So again this is a 'non-problem'. I would assert therefore that there is no problem of viability, as all experience shows. If a country wishes to export all over the world, and import from all over the world, it has never been held that it had to annex the whole world in order to do so.

What about the absolute necessity of having a large internal market? This again is an optical illusion if the meaning of 'large' is conceived in terms of political boundaries. Needless to say, a prosperous market is better than a poor one, but whether that market is outside the political boundaries or inside, makes on the whole very little difference. I am not aware, for instance that Germany, in order to export a large number of Volkswagens to the United States, a very prosperous market, could only do so after annexing the Untied States. But it does make a lot of difference if a poor community or province finds itself politically tied to or ruled by a rich community or province. Why? Because, in a mobile, footloose society the law of disequilibrium is infinitely stronger than the so-called law of equilibrium. Nothing succeeds like success, and nothing stagnates like stagnation. The successful province drains the life out of the unsuccessful, and without protection against the strong, the weak have no chance, either they remain weak or they must migrate and join the strong, they cannot effectively help themselves.

The most important problem in this second half of the Twentieth Century is the geographical distribution of population, the question of 'regionalism'. But regionalism not in the sense of combining a lot of states into free-trade systems, but in the opposite sense of developing all the regions within each country. This, in fact, is the most important subject on the agenda of all the larger countries today. And a lot of the nationalism of small nations today, and the desire for self-government and so-called independence, is simply a logical and rational response to the need for regional development. In the poor countries in particular there is no hope for the poor unless there is successful regional development, a development effort outside the capital city covering all the rural areas wherever people happen to be.

If this effort is not brought forth, their only choice is either to remain in their miserable condition where they are, or to migrate into the big city where their condition will be even more miserable. It is a strange phenomenon indeed that the conventional wisdom of present-day economics can do nothing to help the poor.

Invariably it proves that only such policies are viable as have in fact the result of making those already rich and powerful, richer and more powerful. It proves that economic development only pays if it is as near as possible to the capital city or another very large town, and not in the rural areas. It proves that large projects are invariably more economic than small ones, and it proves that capital-intensive projects are invariably to be preferred as against labour-intensive ones. The economic calculus, as applied by present-day economic forces, compels the industrialist to eliminate the human factor because machines do not make mistakes which people do. Hence the enormous effort at automation and the drive for ever-larger units. This means that those who have nothing to sell but their labour remain in the weakest possible bargaining position. The conventional wisdom of what is now taught as economics by-passes the poor, the very people for whom development is really needed. The economics of giantism and automation are a left-over of Nineteenth Century conditions and Nineteenth Century thinking and they are totally incapable of solving any of the real problems of today. An entirely new system of thought is needed, a system based on attention to people, and not primarily attention to goods – (the goods will look after themselves!). It could be summed up in the phrase, "production by the masses, rather than mass production". What was impossible however in the Nineteenth Century, is possible now. And what was in fact –

if not necessarily at least understandable in the Nineteenth Century is unbelievably urgent now. That is, the conscious utilisation of our enormous technological and scientific potential for the fight against misery and human degradation; that is a fight in intimate contact with actual people, with individuals, families, small groups, rather than states and other anonymous abstractions. And this presupposes a political and organisational structure that can provide this intimacy.

What is the meaning of democracy, freedom, human dignity, standard of living, self-realisation, fulfilment? Is it a matter of goods or of people? Of course it is a matter of people. But people can be themselves only in small comprehensible groups. Therefore we must learn to think in terms of an articulated structure that can cope with a multiplicity of small-scale units. If economic thinking cannot grasp this it is useless. If it cannot get beyond its vast abstractions, the national income, the rate of growth, capital/output ratio, input-output analysis, labour mobility, capital accumulation, if it cannot get beyond all this and make contact with the human realities of poverty, frustration, alienation, despair, breakdown, crime, escapism, stress, congestion, ugliness and spiritual death, then let us scrap economics and start afresh.

Are there not indeed enough 'signs of the times' to indicate that a new start is needed?

Chapter Nine

Disunion Now

Leopold Kohr

We like to believe that the misery into which the world has come is due to the fact that humanity is split into too many countries. And we like to believe that all the evils of our globe would be eliminated by simply doing away with the varieties of states through uniting – the democracies now, the continents later, the world in the end. The usually cited examples for the feasibility of such unions are the United States of America and Switzerland.

As far as the United States is concerned, it is not a model after which Europe could be reshaped because it is not a union of different entities. There is no real differentiation between the peoples, languages, customs and races living in the various states. There is only one people, the American, living in the United States, which is plural in its name but not in fact. The United States are not a country, it *is* a country. The only lesson which can be drawn from its constitutional picture is that, in spite of the uniformity of type it has produced, it was found more practical to subdivide it into 48 states instead of trying to govern the entire continent through delegates from Washington. Thus *differentiations* were artificially created because this proved to be an easier way to achieve union rather than *unification*.

But more than the United States, it is Switzerland which is regarded as the proof of the feasibility of the unionist dreams even for the continent of Europe where they have neither a uniform type of continental man, nor a common language, nor a common cultural and historical background. There, in a tiny spot in the Alps, three arch-enemies – Italians, Germans and French – have united for the common purpose of freedom, peace and economic happiness. Switzerland, to the unionist, is the eternal example of the practicability of the living together of different nations, and, for this reason, he praises her as his holy land.

But in reality Switzerland, too, proves something quite different from what she is meant to prove. The percentage of her national groups (Not speaking of the Romanche, her fourth nationality) is roughly 70 percent for the German, 20 percent for the French and 10 percent for the Italian-speaking population. If these three national groups as such were the basis of her much-famed union, it would inevitably result in the domination of the large German-speaking block over the other two nationalities, who would become degraded to the logical status of minorities representing only 30 percent of the total population. Indeed the rules of democracy would favour this development, and the reason for the French and Italian-speaking communities remaining in a chiefly German enterprise would be gone. No sense could be found in their keeping away from more logical union with their own blood-relatives, who, through their number have formed the powerful nations of Italy and France. No more sense could there be for the Germanic block to stay outside the Reich.

In fact the basis of the existence of Switzerland and the principal of living together of various national groups is not the federation of her three nationalities but the federation of her 22 states, which represent a *division* of her nationalities and thus create the essential precondition for any democratic federation: the physical balance of the participants, the approximate equality of numbers. The greatness of the Swiss idea, therefore, is the smallness of its cells from which it derives its guarantees. The Swiss from Geneva does not confront the Swiss from Zurich as a French to a German confederate from the Republic of Geneva to a confederate from the Republic of Zurich. The citizen of German-speaking Uri is as much a foreigner to the citizen of Italian-speaking Tessin. Between the canton if St. Gallen and the Swiss federation is no intermediary organisation in the form of "German-speaking cantons". The power delegated to Berne derives from the small member republic and not from the nationality, because Switzerland is a union of states, not of nations. It is important to realise that in Switzerland there live (in rough numbers) 700,000 Bernese, 650,000 Zurichois; 160,000 Genevese; etc; and not 2,500,000 Germans; 1,00,000 French and 500,000 Italians. The great number of proud, democratic and almost sovereign cantons, and the small number of the individual cantonal populations eliminates all possible imperialist ambitions on the part of any one canton, because it would always be out-numbered by even a very small combination of others. If ever, in the course of contemporary simplification and rationalism, an attempt to reorganize Switzerland on the basis of its nationalities should succeed, the 22 'superfluous' states with all their separate parliaments and governments would become three provinces: not of Switzerland, however, but of Germany, Italy and France.

People who argue for a union of nations in Europe because they believe that *this* kind of union has been realised and thus proved its practicability in Switzerland, have never based their wonderful schemes on the principal of cantonal or small-state sovereignty. The *national* idea has so much troubled the minds of the political thinkers that, in contrast, the notion of *state*, which is so much more flexible, adaptable and multipliable than that of *nation*, has almost completely gone out of use. For virtue has been seen only in great and greater entities, while smaller entities have been thought and taught to be the source of all mischief and evil. We have been educated in the worship of the bulk, of the large, of the universal, of the colossal, and have come away from the miniscule, the completeness and the universality on the smallest scale – the individual, which is the protoplasm of all social life. We have learned to praise the unification of France, Britain, Italy and Germany in the belief that they would give birth to a unified humanity. But they have created only great powers.

If the Swiss experience should be applied to Europe, also the Swiss technique – not merely the appearance of its result – will have to be employed. This consists in the dividing of three or any number of unequal blocks into as many smaller parts as is necessary to eliminate any sizeable numerical preponderance. That is to say that one should create 40 or 50 equally small states instead of 4 or 5 unequally large ones. Otherwise even a federated Europe will always contain 80 million Germans, 45 million French, 45 million Italians etc, which means that any European federation would end up in a German hegemony with just the same inevitability as the German federation, in which 24 small states were linked to the one 40-million Power of Prussia, ended up in Prussian hegemony.

The suggestion, therefore, is to split Germany up into a number of states of seven to ten million inhabitants. This could be easily done since the former German states (or a number of them) could be reconstructed, and even Prussia could be divided on a natural and historical basis. The splitting up of Germany alone, however, would have no permanent effect. With the natural tendency of all growing things, Germany would reunite unless the whole of Europe were to be cantonised at the same time. France would make the task easy; we shall again have a Venezia, a Lombardy, a Burgundy, a Savoy, an Esthonia, a White Russia, etc. But as with the German states, here also the new (or old) entities would again grow together on racial lines unless they are brought together in *new combinations* making the creation of national states impossible. That is to say, the true meaning of Switzerland or the Austro-Hungarian Empire will have to be realised in many new instances: the small states should be federated, but not with their nearest relative, so that the new map of Europe might show a Pomerania-West-Poland, an East-Prussia-Baltica, an Austria-Hungary-Czechoslovakia, a Baden-Burgundy, a Lombardy-Savoy, etc. Then the Great Powers, which are the womb of all modern wars, because they alone are strong enough to give war its modern frightfulness, shall have disappeared. But only through splitting up the entire continent of Europe will it be possible to eliminate honourably Germany or any other great Power without having to inflict on any of them the odium of a new Versailles. Once Europe is divided into small enough parcels, we shall have the Swiss foundation of a Pan European Union, based not on the collaboration of powerful nations but on the smallness of all of the states.

All this is a defence of the much ridiculed principal which glorifies the sovereignty of the smallest and not of the largest state-entity – *Kleinstaaterie,* as the Germans say. The theorists of our time who only seem to be able to see the large and get emotional over words like "humanity" (no one knows what it really means and why should one *die* for it) call the very idea of creating more instead of fewer states medieval backwardness. They are all out for unionism and colossalism, though unionism is nothing really but another expression for totalitarianism, even if it is thought to be a guarantee for peace. It is the one-party system transplanted into the international field. Against the scorn of our theorists, I would like to point out only a few of the advantages of this "medieval" scheme. The unionist will say that the time when hundreds of states existed was dark and that wars were waged almost continuously. That is true. But what were these wars like? The duke of Tyrol declared war on the Margrave of Bavaria for a stolen horse. The war lasted two weeks. There was one dead and six wounded. A village was captured and all the wine drunk which was in the cellar of the inn. Peace was made and \$35 was paid for reparations. The adjoining Duchy of Liechtenstein and the Archbishop of Salzburg never learned that there had been a war on at all. There was war in some corner of Europe almost every day, but these were wars with relatively little effects. Today we have relatively few wars, and they are for no better reason than a stolen horse. But the effects are tremendous.

Also economically the advantages of the co-existence of many little states were enormous, although the modern synchronisers and economists will not agree with this since they have got accustomed to seeing the world standing on their heads. Instead of one administration we had twenty, instead of two hundred parliamentarians we had two thousand, and, thus, instead of the ambitions of only a few the ambitions of many could be satisfied. There were no unemployed, because there were too many identical professions which competed less because they were exercised in more countries. There was no necessity for socialism (another totalitarian notion), because the economic life of a small country could be supervised from any church tower without the interpretations (brilliant though they be) of a Marx or Schacht. There was the development of the arts in the many capitals which excelled in the creation of universities, theatres and in the production of poets, philosophers and architects. And there were no more taxes than we have now, in the age of rationalism, where people and enterprises have been 'economised' for economic reasons and the phenomenon of unemployment has come into existence. We have done away with what we thought was the waste of courts and kings and have created thereby the splendor of the dictators' marching millions. We have ridiculed the many little states; now we are terrorized by their few successors.

Not only history but our own experience has taught us that true democracy in Europe can only be achieved in little states. Only there the individual can retain his place and dignity. And if democracy is a worthwhile idea, we have to create again the conditions for its development: the small state, and give the glory of sovereignty (instead of curtailing an institution from which no one wants to depart) to the smallest community and to as many as possible. It will be easy to unite *small* states under one continental federal system and thus also satisfy, secondarily, those who want to live on universal terms. Such a Europe is like a fertile inspiration and a grandiose picture, although not a modern one which you paint in one dull line. It will be like a mosaic with fascinating variations and diversity, but also with the harmony of the organic and living whole.

This is a ridiculous scheme, conceived for man as a witty, vivacious and individualistic reality. Unionism, on the other hand is a deadly serious scheme without humour, meant for men as a collectivity and as social animals of lower order; and it reminds me constantly in all its earnest elaborateness, of the German professor who submitted to Satan a new plan for organizing Hell. Whereupon Satan answered with rock-shattering laughter: "Organise, Hell? My dear professor, organization *is* Hell."

First published in 1941 in *The Commonweal*.

Index

Other Books from **New European**

Available to readers at 20% discount.
Send cheques to: New European Publications Limited
14-16 Carroun Road, London SW8 1JT
Tel/Fax ++44 (0) 20 7582 3996

QUESTIONS OF IDENTITY
Exploring the Character of Europe
Edited by Christopher Joyce
ISBN 1-86064-696-4
256 pages   paperback   £14.95
Published in association with IB Tauris.
(Available post free from New European Publications direct.)

What does 'European' mean? European identity has long been hotly
debated and a cause of deep division both in political parties and in Britain
at large. This book brings together powerful and cutting edge contributions
from all sides of the debate over the past three decades from academics,
journalists, business people and politicians. Contributors include Ronald
Butt, Lord Dahrendorf, Richard Hoggart, Flora Lewis, Cees Nooteboom,
Norman Stone and Margaret Thatcher.

A selection of articles from the journal New European. Some radical alternatives for Europe's future.

THE POLITICS OF THE FORKED TONGUE
Authoritarian Liberalism
Aidan Rankin
ISBN 1-8724-1016-2
161 pages   paperback   £13.95

The book is a critique of 'political correctness'. Unlike the standard conservative critiques, it argues that 'PC' harms most those that it aims to
help, such as women and minorities. 'PC' is a symptom of a shift in liberal
thought - from individual freedom to 'group rights'.

THE BREAKDOWN OF EUROPE
Richard Body
ISBN 1-8724-1011-1
101 pages   hardback   £9.95

How the European Union will break down in the electronic age and how the other mega states in the world will also disintegrate.

"Sir Richard Body is the most original thinker in today's Conservative Party."
Aidan Rankin, *Times Literary Supplement*

THE BREAKDOWN OF NATIONS
Leopold Kohr
ISBN 1-870098-98-6
256 pages   paperback   £9.95
(with a foreword by Richard Body and Neil Ascherson)
Published in association with Green Books.
(Available post free from New European Publications direct.)

Leopold Kohr's seminal work which inspired Schumacher and the whole *Small is Beautiful movement*. It argues that people have happier and better lives in smaller states.

"This is the most important work written by the most original thinker of the late 20th century."
Neil Ascherson

EUROPE OF MANY CIRCLES
Constructing a Wider Europe
Richard Body
ISBN 1-8724-1001-4
182 pages   hardback   £14.95

Europe of Many Circles sets out how the European Community can be reshaped into something big enough to serve the people of all Europe, while also small enough in power to allow her people to enjoy both democracy and individual liberty.

"Richard Body's *Europe of Many Circles* is brilliant."
The Telegraph

THE CONSCIENCE OF EUROPE
Edited by John Coleman
ISBN 92-871-4030-8
212 pages   £12.00
Published by the Council of Europe in association with New European Publications

The Council of Europe, which President de Gaulle described as 'that Sleeping Beauty on the banks of the Rhine', is the institution through which the spiritual and moral leadership of Europe should be expressed. Contributors include: Cosmo Russell, Vaclav Havel, Peter Smithers and George Carey.

"The approach to the subject is decidedly spiritual, as befits an examination of conscience, and provides a welcome change from the usual economic or political analyses of the EU..."

Alain Woodrow, *The Tablet*

"Churchmen and statesmen, poets and philosophers, each were asked to contribute a response which might be collated, with the original essay, into a compiled work. The result is truly remarkable - and in truth impossible to review."
James Bourlet, *Britain and Overseas (Economic Research Council)*

"*The conscience of Europe* is a book for both eurosceptics and europhiles. As such I recommend it highly as a means of stimulating the woefully inadequate discussion in Britain about the future of Europe."

Graham Dines, *East Anglia Daily Times*

DISINTEGRATING EUROPE
The Twilight of the European Construction
Noriko Hama
Adamantine Studies on the Changing European Order, No.7
ISBN 0-7449-0122-7
144 pages   hardback   £27.50
ISBN 0-7449-0123-5
144 pages   paperback   £14.50
Published in association with New European Publications.
(Available post free from New European Publications direct.)

"The book has challenged and intensified Japanese interest in Europe's immediate future and opens the way for fresh constructive discussion in Europe itself on how to invigorate the Continent."

George Bull, Editor, *International Minds*

"Presents a clear and exhaustive picture of Europe at a turning-point in its history – the collapse of the post-war system."

Nichi-ei Times

THE THROW THAT FAILED
Britain's 1961 Application to Join the Common Market
Lionel Bell
ISBN 1-8724-1003-0
224 pages   paperback   £15.00

Lionel Bell analyses the until recently secret government papers which are now available under the 30-year rule. With a lifetime of experience in the Public Record Office and elsewhere in the Civil Service, including responsibility for the papers of Winston Churchill, he is in a unique position to assemble and weigh all the evidence relating to this issue, which continues to have such momentous consequences for Europe's future.

ENGLAND FOR THE ENGLISH
Richard Body
ISBN 1-8724-1014-6
181 pages   hardback   £13.95

A provocative and controversial but optimistic book about England's future, now that the United Kingdom is breaking up. The English will prosper and their culture – their core values and beliefs – in the electronic age will make them influential in the world. England will always be multiracial, but her unity and future depends upon rejecting multiculturalism.

"Body's solution seems to be a decentralised Europe less like the US and more like Switzerland.

Aidan Rankin, *Times Literary Supplement*

"Sir Richard Body is a politician of unusual intelligence."

The Daily Telegraph

CHARLEMAGNE
Douglas Pickett / drawings by Harry Tucker
ISBN 1-8724-1002-2
paperback   £2.50

The story of Charlemagne, one of the great Europeans in History, is written for 12-16 year olds but is suitable for all ages.

THE SIMULTANEOUS POLICY
An Insider's Guide to Saving Humanity and the Planet
John Bunzl (with a foreword by Diana Schumacher)
ISBN 1-8724-1015-4
210 pages   hardback   £14.95

The greatest barrier to solving our global environmental, economic and social problems is destructive competition between nations to attract capital and jobs, harming society and the environment around the world.

The Simultaneous Policy offers a solution and also outlines a political campaign that transcends party politics and offers the prospect of global transformation and survival.

"It's ambitious and provocative. Can it work? Certainly worth a serious try."
Noam Chomsky

"It's a good idea. What we need is politicians who will give this issue a high priority."
Polly Toynbee, *The Guardian*

"Your proposal ... reflects the core ideas of how to create consensus around change. This is the biggest challenge that we have."
Ed Mayo, Executive Director, *New Economic Foundation*

SEVEN STEPS TO JUSTICE
Rodney Shakespeare and Peter Challen
ISBN 1-8724-1027-8
212 pages   paperback   £10.95

Seven Steps to Justice is an overall rethinking of economics and politics to create a new paradigm providing two basic incomes for all, a proper deal for both halves of humanity and hope for the world.

TONY BLAIR
Making Labour Liberal
David Wells
ISBN 0-907044-05-1
176 pages   paperback   £5.99
Published in association with Rain Press.
(Available post free from New European Publications direct.)

"An exhilaratingly clear analysis of New Labour's half-baked ideology, and the postmodern authoritarianism of the Blair "Project" ... "
Aidan Rankin, Deputy Editor, *The New European*

"I am normally wary of reading political books because so often they are badly written and full of weak arguments and academic jargon, but your book has none of these failings and I greatly enjoyed its original analysis of Blair as a Liberal."
Leo McKinstry, author and *Daily Mail* feature writer

"The book's critique of what passes for Blair's philosophy is timely and often acute, especially in its relationship with the neo-liberal agenda of economic globalisation."
Brian Fewster, *Green World*, Winter 2000/1, p 20

YUGOSLAVIA – AN AVOIDABLE WAR
Nora Beloff
ISBN 1-8724-1008-1
150 pages plus 16 photographs   paperback   £12.95

In this outstanding appraisal of the modern history of Yugoslavia and the factors surrounding its break-up, Nora Beloff takes sacred tenets of received wisdom and subjects them to close analysis. Interventions by foreign governments, the role of the United Nations, the recognition of the secessionists' political platforms, together with the diplomatic infighting and confusion are all chronicled in this concise account.

NURTURING THE NATURAL LAWS OF PEACE
Through Regional Peace and Development Programmes
ISBN 1-872410-25-1
132 pages   paperback   £10.95

The book is founded on the idea of international law based on co-operation, social, economic and political human rights, as enshrined in the UN Charter. Something like regional Marshall Plans are needed fro the poorer areas of the world, especially today if there is to be any hope of stemming the tide of terrorism.

THE WITHERED GARLAND
Reflections and Doubts of a Bomber
Peter Johnson
ISBN 1-8724-1004-9
370 pages plus photographs   hardback   £20.00

The story of a RAF pilot who commanded Lancaster squadrons in the Second World War who began to doubt the idea that the best way to win wars was to terrorise civilian populations.

"One of the most important books of the twentieth century."   Bruce Kent

RETRIEVED FROM THE FUTURE
John Seymour
ISBN 1-8724-1005-7
235 pages   paperback   £10.00

John Seymour imagines a crash of the structure of Government in Britain and gives a chilling but realistic description of how a federation of East Anglia survives. The recent emergency procedures following the collapse of the South East Asian economies suggest that Seymour is fairly near the mark in his vivid description of life in such circumstances.

COLEMAN'S DRIVE
John Coleman
ISBN 1-8724-1006-5
260 pages plus illustrations   paperback   £10.00

This is the true story of a ride from Buenos Aires to New York in a 1925 Austin 7 'Chummy' through the mountains, deserts and jungles of South and Central America.

"Coleman's Drive with its implied challenge to a classic of travel is, like its author, tough cool and daring."

"His fantastic journey had to be improvised in short stretches of guesswork on the edge of risk."

Times Literary Supplement

"Coleman's book is a fascinating account of a fascinating journey."

The Guardian

"This is one of the best travel books of recent times."

Motor Sport

CHASING GHOSTS
Brian Milton
ISBN 1-8724102-3-5
224 pages   hardback   £16.99

The story of an attempt to cross the Atlantic by Microlight, by the author of the famous *Global Flyer*.

SOD'EM AT GOMORRAH
Chris Wright
ISBN 1-872410-22-7
292 pages   paperback   £12.95

A story that portrays two opposite ways of life and asks the question: which is sustainable?

SCIENCE AND TECHNOLOGY FOR EIGHT BILLION PEOPLE:
Europe's Responsibility
Edited by Peter H. Mettler
Adamantine Studies on the 21st Century, No. 17
ISBN 0-7449-0125-1
333 pages   hardback   £40.00
Published in association with New European Publications. (Available post-free at £19.95 from New European Publications direct.)

Can Europe take the world lead in championing "Science and Technology with a humane agenda"? What are the short, medium, and long-term priorities of such an agenda and how can the global Science & Technology community as a whole best adopt it in order to serve the basic needs and aspirations of the eight billion people who will inhabit the planet by the year 2020?

This book documents and discusses these issues, as raised at the "Europrospective III" conference in Wiesbaden in 1993.